AMATEUR AND FLIRT

Two Screenplays

Hal Hartley

ELBORO

AMATEUR AND FLIRT
Two Screenplays
Copyright © 2022 by Hal Hartley

All rights reserved. No part of this book may be used or reproduced in any manner whatsoever without written permission except in the case of brief quotation embodied in critical articles and reviews.

ISBN: 978-1-7321817-9-3

Published in New York by Elboro Press

Elboro Press books may be purchased in bulk for educational, business or sales promotional use. Please address enquiries to:

office@elboropress.com

First Edition, 2022 – First Printing

AMATEUR

1

FLIRT

103

These revised and corrected versions of *Amateur* (originally written in 1993) and *Flirt* (written in parts between 1993 and 1995) are based on Hal Hartley's original scripts and notes. Both screenplays deviate in small ways from the films that were eventually produced and released.

Amateur

01. EXTERIOR, ALLEY—DAY

A well-dressed man, Thomas, is lying, apparently lifeless, on the cobblestones of this dim and unused backstreet. A young woman, Sofia, appears from around a corner, breathless and frightened. She approaches the body and sees a small pool of blood beneath the head. She nudges the corpse with her foot, then backs away, glancing around to see if anyone has witnessed this. Seeing no one, she turns and runs away. Dirty rain water streams past the body. A breeze sweeps over Thomas and he slowly revives and opens his eyes. He tries to sit up but it hurts too much and so he lies back and catches his breath.

                        ISABELLE
                (off)
          And this man will die. He will. Eventually.

02. INTERIOR, COFFEE SHOP—DAY

Isabelle is a pale young woman sitting at the counter and writing on a laptop. She is pretty, but plain and simply dressed. She types feverishly, reciting aloud as she composes, unaware of the other customers.

                        ISABELLE
          "He will die," she repeated, "and there is
          nothing any of us can do about it." Vera put
          the last of the bullets into the chamber of the
          gun and stood in the window to keep an eye
          on the street below. Frank's calloused hand
          worked its way up under her tight-fitting
          skirt and caressed her perfect ass. He pulled
          her back against himself and she felt his cock
          against her, like a piece of two-by-four in his
          trousers.

                        CUSTOMER
          Listen, lady, you better settle down! You're
          embarrassing my friend!

Isabelle hasn't heard the irate woman and leans forward over the counter with her cup.

ISABELLE

Excuse me, can I have another coffee, please?

WAITRESS

You can't sit here all day, you know!

ISABELLE
(meekly)

But I pay for my coffee.

WAITRESS

You buy one or two cups of coffee and you sit there all day! Day after day! You take up space!

ISABELLE

I bought one of those muffins this morning.

WAITRESS

You did not.

ISABELLE

I did.

WAITRESS

Which kind?

ISABELLE
(points)

That kind.

FRANK
(the cook at the grill)

Ah, leave her alone! She's harmless!

WAITRESS

This is not a hotel!

ISABELLE

It had mold on it.

But everyone now turns to watch Thomas limp in through the door, dazed, bloody, the pocket of his jacket torn half off.

> WAITRESS
> *(unwelcoming)*
> Can I help you?

But Thomas can't find the words to answer and he looks around, lost.

> WAITRESS
> *(continues)*
> Come on, pal, what'll it be!

He finds some change in his jacket pocket and dumps it all on the counter. The waitress lifts one of the coins and frowns at him.

> WAITRESS
> *(of coin)*
> This is no good. What kind of money is this? What kind of money is this, Frank?

> FRANK
> *(looks)*
> Dutch.

> WAITRESS
> *(to Thomas)*
> Are you Dutch?

> THOMAS
> Maybe...

> FRANK
> He sounds like an American.

> WAITRESS
> Where'd you get this Dutch money?

> THOMAS
> It was... in my... pocket.

WAITRESS
Look, take your Dutch money and get outta here!

ISABELLE
He's hurt.

WAITRESS
Are you still here?

ISABELLE
(approaches)
He's bleeding. Bring some water.
(to Thomas)
Does it hurt?

THOMAS
I guess so...

WAITRESS
(brings water)
What's your name?

THOMAS
I... don't know.

ISABELLE
(cleans his head wound)
Keep still.

WAITRESS
Frank, he doesn't know his name.

ISABELLE
Are you hungry?

THOMAS
(looks at his hands)
Yes. Maybe. Where am I?

Isabelle removes a few dollars from her bag and hands it across the counter.

>   ISABELLE
> A sandwich, please.

>   WAITRESS
> Hey, look, Frank, she's got actual money!

03. INTERIOR, COFFEE SHOP—DAY

Later, Isabelle watches Thomas finish eating his sandwich as he reads what she's written on her laptop.

>   ISABELLE
> Did you have enough to eat?

>   THOMAS
> Yes. Thank you. You want some?

>   ISABELLE
> No.

>   THOMAS
> You sure?

>   ISABELLE
> Yes. Do you smoke?

>   THOMAS
> I don't know.

She taps a cigarette out from the pack she has.

>   ISABELLE
> I just started smoking. It helps me forget I'm hungry.

>   THOMAS
> Well, then eat some of this.

She looks at the sandwich and shakes her head.

ISABELLE
No, I couldn't.

THOMAS
Why not?

ISABELLE
I'm not hungry.

THOMAS
You're only forgetting you're hungry because of the cigarettes.

ISABELLE
Yes, I know. But I had a muffin too.

THOMAS
When?

ISABELLE
(evasive)
Before.

Isabelle sits down closer to him.

THOMAS
I was reading your story.

ISABELLE
Did you like it?

THOMAS
It's sad.

ISABELLE
Yes, everything I write comes out sad. Why do you think that is?

THOMAS
(firmly)
I don't know. Look, eat this.

And he places the sandwich before her as he takes her cigarettes. After a little hesitation, Isabelle takes a bite. Satisfied, Thomas grabs the matches off the counter.

            ISABELLE
You have no identification?

            THOMAS
No. I woke up in the street and I don't know how I got there.

Excited, Isabelle begins to have story ideas.

            ISABELLE
Perhaps you were robbed!

            THOMAS
Could be.

            ISABELLE
Maybe you tried to commit suicide!

            THOMAS
    (smokes)
You think so?

            ISABELLE
    (notices)
You know how.

            THOMAS
How to what, commit suicide?

            ISABELLE
No. You know how to smoke. It took me a few weeks to learn how to inhale. But it comes very natural to you.

            THOMAS
    (studies cigarette)
Did I inhale?

                    ISABELLE
    Yes.

                    THOMAS
              (of sandwich)
    Eat that.

She rolls her eyes petulantly and continues eating.

                    ISABELLE
    And you're naturally bossy. You're a criminal
    of some kind, I think.

                    THOMAS
            (reads ad on matchbook)
    "Hot Phone Sex."

                    ISABELLE
              (of matches)
    You can keep them if you want.

He puts the matches in his pocket and notices the small stack of magazines beside her laptop.

                    THOMAS
    What are these?

                    ISABELLE
    Pornographic magazines.

                    THOMAS
               (lifts one)
    May I?

                    ISABELLE
    Sure. I met this man, George, who says he'll
    pay me to write some of these short stories
    they publish.

Thomas flips through one of the magazines and finds just such a story. He reads:

                THOMAS
"He reached out a hand and grabbed her chin,
forcing his fingers brutally into her cheeks as
he lifted her face towards his. 'I never use
the same woman twice,' he said, 'any more
than I'd smoke the same cigarette twice.
You're used up. I've gotten all I need or want
out of you.'"
        (to Isabelle)
That ever happen to you?

                ISABELLE
        (blinks, looks away)
No. I'm afraid not.

04. EXTERIOR, COFFEE SHOP—MOMENTS LATER

Isabelle is throwing up in the alley out back. Thomas stands aside with her laptop and sweater. The waitress rides by on her bike, leaving work, calling back over her shoulder:

                WAITRESS
She never eats anything! That's what the
problem is!

                THOMAS
Thank you!

                WAITRESS
You gotta have some food in your gut to
build up resistance to the heat and humidity!

                THOMAS
Right.

Isabelle is through being sick. She leans against a wall and then starts walking along.

                ISABELLE
        (to Thomas)
I'm sorry.

THOMAS
What for?

ISABELLE
I should go back to the convent.

THOMAS
You're a nun?

ISABELLE
No. Not anymore.

He pauses and watches her walk on. He still has her things. He follows.

05. INTERIOR, ISABELLE'S PLACE—DAY

It's a small, poor place. Isabelle comes in, sick and cold, and falls upon the bed. Thomas follows her in and closes the door. She gets right back up, not letting herself rest.

ISABELLE
I have some antiseptic for your cuts.

She steps into the bathroom.

ISABELLE
Can you remember anything at all about who you are?

He sits and thinks.

THOMAS
I feel things. But I don't know what they mean.
No. I don't remember. I'm confused, mostly.

ISABELLE
Are you frightened?

THOMAS
Frightened?

ISABELLE

Yes, scared.

THOMAS

Of what?

ISABELLE

I don't know.

She goes to the door, sets the heavy chain lock, then looks back at Thomas and pauses.

ISABELLE

So you don't remember anything? No feelings, no caresses, no kisses, no...

THOMAS

No.

Isabelle considers this. She looks at her wristwatch.

ISABELLE

I have a date.

THOMAS
(stands)
Yeah. I should go. Thank you.

ISABELLE

No. Don't leave. We can go to the police in the morning. You can stay here tonight.

THOMAS
(looks around at the small room)
Alright. I'll sleep on the floor.

ISABELLE

No.

THOMAS

I don't mind.

> ISABELLE
> I have no blankets for you if you sleep on
> the floor.

> THOMAS
> I'll use my jacket.

> ISABELLE
> But you can sleep in the bed with me.

He looks at the bed and then at her.

> THOMAS
> There's no room in the bed for the two of us.

> ISABELLE
> There is. If we lie very close together.

> THOMAS
> Who do you have a date with?

> ISABELLE
> I don't know. His name is Warren. I've only
> spoken to him on the hot phone sex party line.

06. INTERIOR, MOVIE THEATER—DAY

A pornographic film is in progress. Isabelle enters with Warren. As they find a seat, Isabelle notices Sofia asleep across the aisle. Her purse has dropped to the floor. Isabelle retrieves it and places it back in her lap. Just then, the usher approaches and shines a flashlight at the sleeping girl. She wakes with a start.

> USHER
> Hey. Hey, come on. Get up.

Sofia wakes with a start and looks up at him, terrified.

> USHER
> This is not a hotel. You've been in here all day.
> Get up and get outta here!

Sofia pulls herself together, still half asleep.

> ISABELLE
> But there are so many seats here no one is sitting in.

> USHER
> Listen, lady, mind your own business!

She watches as the usher walks Sofia out of the theater. Then she notices Warren has his hand on her thigh.

> ISABELLE
> What are you doing?

> WARREN
> I'm molesting you.

> ISABELLE
> Am I supposed to like it?

> WARREN
> *(excited)*
> You could beg me to stop.

> ISABELLE
> And would you?

> WARREN
> *(very entertained)*
> Probably not. No.

> ISABELLE
> I have to go.

And she gets up and runs out.

07. EXTERIOR, MOVIE THEATER—DAY

Sofia is in a phone booth listening to a dial tone. She looks over as Isabelle comes out of the movie theater. Their eyes meet but both quickly look away. Isabelle walks off. Sofia hangs up.

08. EXTERIOR, CLUB—NIGHT

James is a wiry twenty-five-year-old kid working the door. A female rock fan hands him cash to enter the dark cavern of pulsating noise.

                    JAMES
Thank you.
          (stamps the wrist)
Enjoy.

Sofia comes up and walks back and forth in front of the entrance. James watches her, checking her out. She's aware of this, waits, then comes closer.

                    SOFIA
Who's playing?

                    JAMES
Some band from Seattle.

                    SOFIA
Are they good?

                    JAMES
I guess. I can't hear too well.

                    SOFIA
You must get bored out here.

                    JAMES
I only have to work the door till midnight.

Some students come up and start reaching for their wallets. Sofia steps aside and let's James do his job.

                    JAMES
Have your ID ready please. Thanks.
Thank you. Enjoy the show.

The students file in and, when the door closes, James and Sofia are left alone again.

> JAMES
> You wanna see the show?

> SOFIA
> I can't afford ten dollars.

> JAMES
> Here. Go in anyway.

He takes his little stamp pad and brands the back of her hand.

> SOFIA
> Thank you.

> JAMES
> It's okay. The management wants a lot of good-looking women in the place. It's good for business.

She looks at the little stamp on her wrist, smokes, then—

> SOFIA
> I know.

She enters.

09. INTERIOR, ISABELLE'S PLACE—NIGHT

Thomas is in the bathtub flipping through a pornographic magazine. Isabelle returns, frustrated, and stands in the bathroom door.

> THOMAS
> How was your date?

> ISABELLE
> I think there's something wrong with me.

Thomas closes the magazine and throws it on the floor.

THOMAS
How long has it been since you left the convent, Isabelle?

ISABELLE
Ten months.

THOMAS
How long were you a nun?

ISABELLE
Fifteen years.

THOMAS
That's a long time.

She steps into the bathroom and takes out her cigarettes.

ISABELLE
When I make mistakes, they tend to be big ones.

THOMAS
Were you always religious?

ISABELLE
No.

She lights a cigarette.

ISABELLE
When I was a girl, I wasted a lot of time writing bad poetry about being lonely and too fat.

THOMAS
You were fat, huh?

ISABELLE
Not so fat. But I was ugly. Well, anyway, it was around that time that the Virgin Mary

began appearing to me.

                    THOMAS
             (surprised, uncertain)
Pardon me?

                    ISABELLE
It's true. She appeared to me three times in one year.

                    THOMAS
And what did she say?

                    ISABELLE
She said I should *not* become a nun.

                    THOMAS
Why?

                    ISABELLE
Because I'm a nymphomaniac.

                    THOMAS
Is that so?

                    ISABELLE
It's true.

                    THOMAS
You don't look like one.

                    ISABELLE
Like a nymphomaniac?

                    THOMAS
Yeah.

                    ISABELLE
How would you know?

She's got a point. Thomas looks away and thinks about it.

ISABELLE
But I lied. I told the priest God wanted me to join the order and become a nun.

THOMAS
After all that?

ISABELLE
Well, I was scared.

THOMAS
Of what?

ISABELLE
I was scared of what I knew God had planned for me.

THOMAS
God had something planned for you?

ISABELLE
Yes.

THOMAS
What?

ISABELLE
I don't know yet. The Virgin didn't tell me that. But she did say it's going to be difficult. It's going to hurt. And I need to be out here in the world to do it. Not in a convent.
(sits on edge of tub, smokes)
I was seventeen. I was scared. So I lied. I lied for fifteen years. I lied until I couldn't bear it any longer.

THOMAS
(impressed)
Shit.

Isabelle looks at him, at his body there in the soapy water.

ISABELLE
Will you make love to me?

THOMAS
When?

ISABELLE
When you finish your bath.

THOMAS
Why me?

ISABELLE
Why not you?

THOMAS
Well, you don't know me. You don't even know my name.

ISABELLE
You don't know your name either.

THOMAS
Have you ever had sex?

ISABELLE
No.

THOMAS
How can you be a nymphomaniac and never had sex?

ISABELLE
(smokes, then)
I'm choosy.

THOMAS
I need to shave.

She reaches up and over to the sink and gets him a plastic disposable razor from the medicine cabinet.

                    ISABELLE
          Is this okay? I use it on my legs.

Thomas takes it and lathers up. She watches him. After a while, he glances over at her.

                    THOMAS
          I don't think you're a nymphomaniac.

                    ISABELLE
          You don't?

                    THOMAS
          No.

                    ISABELLE
          And so, you'll make love to me anyway?

He cuts himself shaving and winces in pain.

                    ISABELLE
          I did the same thing yesterday. Here.

She shows him a cut on her leg, up above her knee. He looks at it, then up at her.

                    THOMAS
          I think I'm in too much pain to make love
          tonight.

                    ISABELLE
                    (shrugs)
          I can wait. I've waited all my life.

10. INTERIOR, JAMES'S PLACE—DAY

The next morning, James is still asleep on a mattress on the floor of his tiny one-room apartment. Sofia sits at the edge of the mattress, lacing up her boots. She gets up and grabs the phone. Stepping into the bathroom, she closes the door and dials. This time, her call is answered.

                    SOFIA
                (whispers)
        Edward? It's Sofia. Yes, I'm here in New
        York. I can't talk now. Can I see you?
                (listen, then)
        No.
                (listens again, then)
        Thomas is dead.

11. INTERIOR, ISABELLE'S PLACE—DAY

Thomas is sleeping. Isabelle is sitting up at the edge of the bed looking down upon him, holding a cup of coffee. After watching him a few moments, she reaches out and caresses his shoulder. He jumps up, startled, and Isabelle jumps back in alarm. He gradually realizes where he is and relaxes.

                    THOMAS
        Sorry.

He sits up with his back against the wall.

                    ISABELLE
        You talk in your sleep.

                    THOMAS
        I do?

                    ISABELLE
        Yes.

                    THOMAS
        What do I say?

                    ISABELLE
                (evades this, standing)
        Have some coffee.

                    THOMAS
                (insists)
        What did I say?

ISABELLE
(sits again)
You were shouting at someone named Sofia.

THOMAS
Sofia?

ISABELLE
Do you remember her?

THOMAS
No.

ISABELLE
How do you feel?

THOMAS
A little better.

ISABELLE
Good.

THOMAS
We should go to the police.

ISABELLE
No. Why?

THOMAS
Someone's probably looking for me.

ISABELLE
This Sofia person maybe?

THOMAS
Yeah. Maybe.

ISABELLE
(carefully)
You were very mean to her. I doubt she'd miss you.

                    THOMAS
                (worried)
            Oh, yeah?

                    ISABELLE
            Yes. Very mean.

                    THOMAS
            How?

Isabelle takes another sip of coffee, afraid to answer this. But—

                    ISABELLE
            You were threatening to hurt her.

                    THOMAS
            What did I say?
                (no response, then...)
            Isabelle, what did I say in my sleep?

                    ISABELLE
            You said you were going to slice up her face
            with a razor blade.

Thomas is stunned. Isabelle looks away.

12. INTERIOR, CAFE—DAY

Sofia is sitting at a table talking to Edward, an accountant in a business suit.

                    SOFIA
            I hate him. He took advantage of me. He got
            me hooked on drugs when I was twelve. He
            put me in pornographic films. I'm sick of it.
            I want to change my life. He won't let me.
            I'm unhappy. I pushed him out a window.
            I killed him.

                    EDWARD
            When was this?

SOFIA
Yesterday morning.

EDWARD
Here in New York?

SOFIA
Yes.

EDWARD
How did he know you were in New York?

SOFIA
I don't know. He knew everything.

EDWARD
What did he want?

SOFIA
He was angry because I left him. He said if I didn't come back he was going to disfigure me. He showed me some pictures.
(she shrugs)
Stuff they do to girls.

Edward watches her and sighs, demoralized, then looks away, thinking.

EDWARD
What are you gonna do?

SOFIA
I don't know.
(sits forward, then)
Tell me about Jacques.

EDWARD
Jacques?

SOFIA
Yes.

EDWARD
How do you know about Jacques?

SOFIA
Thomas mentioned him.

EDWARD
Oh, yeah, what did he say?

SOFIA
Not much. But I know Thomas got money from him to make the movies.

Edward is reluctant. He sits back and looks into the street.

EDWARD
He's a businessman.

SOFIA
What did you do for him?

EDWARD
Look, I didn't do anything for him! I'm an accountant! I took care of Thomas's money!

SOFIA
Is what Jacques does illegal?

EDWARD
Look, the less you know about Jacques the better. Forget anything Thomas said about Jacques.

SOFIA
I think Thomas was in trouble with Jacques.

EDWARD
Yeah, Thomas was in trouble with everyone.

SOFIA
Why?

EDWARD
Because he's the devil.

SOFIA
No, I mean why was he in trouble with Jacques?

EDWARD
Thomas tried to blackmail him.

SOFIA
With what?

EDWARD
Accounting documents. Records of banking transactions. Stuff like that.

SOFIA
So Jacques did something illegal?

EDWARD
He's an arms dealer.

SOFIA
And that's not allowed?

EDWARD
It depends. Not always. In this case, definitely not.

SOFIA
What do the documents look like?

EDWARD
Why, do you know where they are?

SOFIA
I don't know.

EDWARD
They're floppy disks.

SOFIA
Floppy disks.

EDWARD
Yeah, you know, like...
(takes one from his case)
Like this.

She takes it and studies it.

SOFIA
This is what you call a floppy disk?

EDWARD
Yeah.

SOFIA
But it's square.

EDWARD
Yeah, yeah, I know, but they call them floppy disks.

SOFIA
It's not floppy either. It's stiff.

EDWARD
(annoyed)
Look, Sofia, did you ever see Thomas with anything that looks like this?

SOFIA
(gives it back)
No.

His cellular phone rings and he answers.

EDWARD
Hello. Yeah. What? No way. Right.
(stands)
I'll be right back.

He goes out on the sidewalk. Sofia waits till he's far enough off then reaches into his briefcase, pokes around a little, then finds what she's looking for: his phone book. Flipping through it, she finds Jacques's number. She copies it down onto a napkin and replaces the phone book. Edward returns. As he sits, he takes out his pen and notepad.

                    EDWARD
Sorry about that.

                    SOFIA
So, what do you do now that you're back in
the States?

                    EDWARD
             (taking out his wallet)
I prepare people's taxes.

                    SOFIA
             (brightly)
Oh, that sounds so interesting!

He glances at her in disbelief as he begins to write in his notepad.

                    EDWARD
Look, this is the address of a house one of my
clients owns upstate in a town called Portchester.
No one's there. You go by train this afternoon,
take a taxi from the station, pick up some
groceries to last a couple of days...
             (gives her money)
Get there and stay put till we see what happens.

                    SOFIA
How will I get in?

                    EDWARD
I'll get the key from my office and meet you
at Grand Central Station.

She leans over and gives him a kiss.

                    SOFIA
Thank you, Edward. I know you must not
think that much of me.

                    EDWARD
No. You're wrong. Anyone who would kill
Thomas is a friend of mine. He's ruined our
lives.

                    SOFIA
No, he hasn't. He damaged them. But I'm
going to change all that. I'm going to change
my life. And I'll help you too. I'm going to
take charge of things. I'm going to be a mover
and a shaker. You wait and see.

13. INTERIOR, POLICE STATION—DAY

Thomas has his picture taken. Afterwards, Officer Melville, a sensitive and emotional woman, tries to reassure him.

                    MELVILLE
That's all we can do for the time being.
No one has reported a person fitting your
description as missing. But if they do, at
least now we have your picture.
        (sighs sadly)
Do you have a place to stay?

                    THOMAS
Yes. Thank you.

                    MELVILLE
        (relieved)
Oh, good. I hate to have to bring people in
your position across the street to the hospital.
It's so cold and unfeeling over there. So
hopeless and, frankly, understaffed.

Her immediate superior, a tough and busy detective, calls from across the room—

CABAN
Let's go, Melville! Don't start crying!

MELVILLE
Okay! Okay!

CABAN
You're an officer of the law, goddammit!

She controls herself and looks back at Thomas.

MELVILLE
Take care. Good luck.

THOMAS
Thank you.

But she runs out into the hall and cries.

14. INTERIOR, CAFE—DAY

Sofia sashays up to the counter and gets the attention of the bartender. He's attracted. She lays her hand on his.

SOFIA
Hello, may I use your phone?

BARTENDER
There's a pay phone by the restroom.

SOFIA
Yes, I know. But I have no change.

BARTENDER
Is it a local call?

SOFIA
(smiles adorably)
Not really, but I'll be brief.

Moments later, she has the phone, steps away, dials, waits—

SOFIA
Hello, I'd like to call the Netherlands.

OPERATOR
What is the number, please?

SOFIA
31 20 646 1155

She waves to the bartender as she waits and is finally connected.

RECEPTIONIST
(Dutch)
Good afternoon. Bad Organization.

SOFIA
Hello. May I speak to Mister Jacques please?

RECEPTIONIST
(English)
Who may I say is calling?

SOFIA
You can tell him Sofia Ludens is calling.

She waits. Eventually, Jacques picks up.

JACQUES
Yes?

SOFIA
Is this Mister Jacques?

JACQUES
Who is this?

SOFIA
This is Sofia Ludens. I'm Thomas's wife.

JACQUES
I know who you are.

SOFIA
So, is this Mister Jacques?

JACQUES
That depends.

SOFIA
On what?

JACQUES
Is Thomas with you?

SOFIA
(hesitates)
No.

JACQUES
Where are you calling from?

SOFIA
I can't tell you that.

JACQUES
Why are you calling, Sofia?

SOFIA
(prepares herself, then)
I need to tell Mister Jacques something important.

JACQUES
Can you tell me?

SOFIA
Are you Mister Jacques?

JACQUES
Yes.

SOFIA
(blinks, confounded)
But how do I know that?

                    JACQUES
You have no choice.

She lowers the receiver and looks away, frustrated. Then—

                    SOFIA
Look, I have something that belongs to Mister
Jacques.

                    JACQUES
Like what?

She breathes deep and finally manages to mumble—

                    SOFIA
Floppy disks.

Silence. She waits. She looks at the receiver. But there is still no response. Finally—

                    JACQUES
What do you want, Sofia?

She thinks quickly, desperately, then—

                    SOFIA
Money. A million dollars.

                    JACQUES
Okay.

Her jaw drops. She lowers the phone and looks at it again.

                    JACQUES
Can you come here to our offices?

                    SOFIA
No. No. I'm not in Amsterdam.

                    JACQUES
It doesn't matter. We have satellite offices

all over the world.

>   SOFIA
> Somewhere public.

>   JACQUES
> Do you have the floppy disks with you?

>   SOFIA
> No, but I can tell you where they are.

>   JACQUES
> Fine. But where do we find you?

She hesitates, trying to think.

>   SOFIA
> New York City.

>   JACQUES
> Where in New York City?

She looks around, exhausted, but then decides.

>   SOFIA
> Grand Central Station.

15. EXTERIOR, STREET—DAY

Thomas is troubled. Isabelle is too. They walk awhile, but then she stops.

>   ISABELLE
> What will you do when you find out who you are?

>   THOMAS
> I can't say.

>   ISABELLE
> You have a little scar here, just above your eye.

> THOMAS
> I do?

> ISABELLE
> I like it.

> THOMAS
> Thanks.

> ISABELLE
> You have to make love to me before you remember your name.

> THOMAS
> Well, I feel a little better today. Why don't we go back to your place and make love right now?

> ISABELLE
> I have to go read my short story to George the pornographer.

> THOMAS
> What about me?

> ISABELLE
> Would you like to look at one of my porno magazines?

She gives him one. He flips through it, bored.

> THOMAS
> Thanks.

> ISABELLE
> Meet me outside my building at five.

16. INTERIOR, GRAND CENTRAL STATION—DAY

Sofia comes skipping across the main concourse of the station, tossing her head to the music on her Walkman. Moments later, she enters the cafe which overlooks the station and finds Edward.

> SOFIA

Hello!

> EDWARD

You're in a good mood.

> SOFIA
> *(gives him flowers)*

Yes. I am in a good mood. These are for you.

Sofia moves aside and observes a man in a business suit standing in the station entrance. He is wearing dark glasses and carrying a briefcase. She waits for him to notice her. He does, but then looks away, uninterested. He is then met by a woman, removes his dark glasses, and kisses her affectionately. They move off. Relieved and disappointed, Sofia sighs and returns to Edward.

> EDWARD
>
> By the way, Sofia, if anyone asks about those floppy disks, or mentions Mister Jacques, you just make like you never heard about any of it. Okay?

> SOFIA

Sure.

> EDWARD
>
> I mean, not even to your closest friend.

> SOFIA
> *(smiles)*

You're my closest friend.

> EDWARD
> *(genuine, flattered)*

Thank you.

> SOFIA
>
> Besides, I'm good at keeping secrets.

EDWARD
That's good.

SOFIA
I learned all sorts of criminal-type behavior from Thomas.

EDWARD
Oh yeah, like what?

She almost recites a list but then changes her mind.

SOFIA
I'd rather not talk about it. It was pretty disgusting.

EDWARD
How did you meet Thomas, anyway?

SOFIA
Through my sister. She used to travel around with these rock'n'roll bands. I left home and joined her.

EDWARD
You were a groupie?

SOFIA
Yes. But then my sister died of an overdose and the band threw me off the bus in the middle of nowhere. That's when I met Thomas and he got me into the movie thing.

EDWARD
And you were twelve years old then?

SOFIA
Almost thirteen.

Edward sits back, a little drunk, sadly fascinated by his own history.

EDWARD
We were good pornographers there for a while.
At least, I thought so. Had offices in London,
Amsterdam, and Miami. We made a product
of a certain quality, paid our bills on time,
made profits. We got rich, actually.

SOFIA
What made you quit?

EDWARD
I had no choice. I was trying to save my life.

SOFIA
I don't understand.

EDWARD
It's true. Jacques will kill anyone who even
knows about those floppy disks.

SOFIA
(quietly startled)
Oh.

EDWARD
I tried to tell Thomas this. I tried to tell him
he was risking my life as well as his own.
Risking your life. Risking the lives of
everybody who worked with us. But he didn't
care. He didn't care about anybody.

SOFIA
(hopefully)
But they didn't kill you.

EDWARD
They didn't kill me because they don't know
where I am.

Terrified now, her mind is racing, Sofia stands up and prepares to leave. She grabs Edward's hand.

SOFIA
We should go now.

EDWARD
I'll walk you to the train.

SOFIA
No. I'm okay. Go home.

EDWARD
I don't want to go home. I'm enjoying myself.

SOFIA
You've got to go home, Edward. You should be hiding.

EDWARD
Ah, they still think I'm in Europe.

Sofia is watching the station entrance. She comes back and leans her body against Edward's.

SOFIA
Come with me, then.

EDWARD
(shyly aroused)
Yeah?

SOFIA
Come with me to the country.

EDWARD
Now?

SOFIA
Yes. Now. Come on, we've got to hurry!

Glancing over, she now sees two particular men, Jan and Kurt, alert and threatening, standing in the station entrance and searching the crowd.

SOFIA
(pleads with Edward)
Aren't we having a good time?

EDWARD
Yeah, yeah, we're having a great time.

SOFIA
I feel so close to you all of a sudden. Please come with me.

EDWARD
Well, sure... But...

SOFIA
Good! Let's go!

She grabs his briefcase and starts to lead him away. But Edward hangs back, conflicted.

EDWARD
There really are one or two things I should take care of at the office before I go.

Now, however, Sofia sees the two men grab a young woman who looks fairly like her—the same haircut and coloring. They turn the terrified young woman around, see it's not Sofia, and let her go. Meanwhile, Edward straightens his tie and prepares to leave.

EDWARD
I'll call you at the house as soon as I can.

He kisses her lightly on the cheek and leaves with the flowers she bought him. Before exiting, he pauses in the station entrance and looks back at her, smitten. Horrified, Sofia runs through the cafe's kitchen and out into an alley in back.

17. EXTERIOR, GRAND CENTRAL STATION—DAY

Edward sits into a cab and reconsiders. The driver waits for instructions, gets none, then looks back over his shoulder.

                    DRIVER
     Where to, pal?

18. INTERIOR, GRAND CENTRAL STATION—DAY

Jan reconnoiters the cafe then steps back over and meets Kurt at the entrance just as Edward walks right by them, returning to join Sofia. Jan, the senior of the two, hits Kurt in the arm and they move off after Edward.

19. EXTERIOR, GRAND CENTRAL STATION—DAY

Sofia runs out from the alley and sees the taxi stand. She jumps into the cab Edward just left.

                    SOFIA
              (breathless)
     Drive.

                    DRIVER
     Where to?

                    SOFIA
              (screams)
     Just drive!

                    DRIVER
     Right.

And the cab drives away just as Edward comes running back out of the station, Jan and Kurt in pursuit. Sofia looks back in horror as Kurt catches up with him and throws Edward against the side of a parked car. Jan catches up and the two of them drag Edward away. Sofia turns forward again, trembling, hangs her head, and covers her face with her hands.

                    ISABELLE
              (off)
     In even the smallest thing, she saw the
     pointlessness of hope, the impossibility of
     forgiveness.

20. INTERIOR, GEORGE'S OFFICE—DAY

George is the editor-in-chief of a popular pornographic magazine. He looks on, troubled, as Isabelle finishes reading her latest story.

                    ISABELLE
                     (reads)
          How is it possible, she asked, that in a universe
          sustaining such conscientious brutality, a friend
          can laugh, a mother smile, a father sacrifice,
          or a lover kiss?

She lowers the pages and looks to George.

                    GEORGE
          Is that it?

                    ISABELLE
          Yes.

He looks away, stands, goes to the window, speechless.

                    ISABELLE
                     (anxious)
          What do you think?

                    GEORGE
          Well, frankly, Isabelle, it's quite bad.

                    ISABELLE
                     (stunned)
          It is?

                    GEORGE
          I'm afraid so.

                    ISABELLE
          But what's wrong with it?

                    GEORGE
          It's not pornographic.

ISABELLE
Yes, it is!
(then, less certain)
The first part is!

GEORGE
It's poetry and don't you try and deny it!

She falls back in her seat, defeated.

ISABELLE
I'm sorry. I've failed you.

GEORGE
Easy. A mistake is not necessarily a failure, Isabelle.

ISABELLE
No?

Georges paces the office, ruminating.

GEORGE
Look at me. I'm a fairly successful editor of dirty magazines. I never intended this. My aspiration was defamatory journalism. My big ambition in life was to get my hands on smutty pictures of the president's mistress. I wanted to undermine huge corporations, sow the seeds of revolt by publishing the sordid details of high-level government corruption.
(sighs, cleans his glasses)
But, you know, things happen. We drift away from our vocation.
(sits beside her and takes money from his wallet)
Now, look, here's a hundred bucks. If you think up something really dirty, really perverse—I mean, really disgusting and gross—give me a call. Okay?

She hesitates, then takes the money.

> ISABELLE
>
> Okay.

21. EXTERIOR, PARK—DAY

Killing time, Thomas comes along and sits on a park bench. There is a twelve-year-old kid, Simon, sitting there reading *The Odyssey* of Homer.

> THOMAS
> *(nods)*
> Hey.

> SIMON
> Hi.

> THOMAS
> What's that you're reading?

> SIMON
> *The Odyssey*.

> THOMAS
> Is it interesting?

> SIMON
> *(glad to discuss)*
> Sort of.

> THOMAS
> What's it about?

> SIMON
> Well, it's about this guy Odysseus mostly. He's king of this place called Ithaca. He's an okay guy. But he has to go and fight in this war and he's gone for ten years. And then, on the way back, he gets lost and he's wandering around for another ten years.

THOMAS
Wow.

SIMON
And he's got this really beautiful wife, Penelope, back home. All the other men in Ithaca want to marry her.

THOMAS
Can I see it?

Simon hands him the book and Thomas looks around in it while Simon continues.

SIMON
But Penelope doesn't want to marry any of them because she's waiting for Odysseus to get back. But, for all she knows, he could be dead.

THOMAS
(hands back book)
Sounds great.

SIMON
What are you reading?

Thomas sees he means the magazine in his jacket pocket. He pulls it out and hands it to Simon.

THOMAS
Chicks.

Simon flips through the current issue of *Chicks* with great interest.

THOMAS
Do you find those women attractive?

SIMON
(compares a few, then)
I prefer girls my own age.

                    THOMAS
That's understandable.

                    SIMON
Do all women have hair between their legs
like this?

                    THOMAS
Yeah, I guess. Most. There's a woman on
page twenty-two who doesn't.

Simon flips back to page twenty-two and checks this out.

                    SIMON
Can I keep this?

                    THOMAS
It belongs to a friend of mine. I gotta give it back.

                    SIMON
                (turns page)
Look, a new Sofia Ludens movie!

Thomas looks on, alarmed by the reoccurrence of Sofia's name.

                    THOMAS
Who?

                    SIMON
Sofia Ludens.

Simon shows him the page.

                    THOMAS
Who is it?

                    SIMON
                (enthusiastic)
She's the most notorious porn actress in the
world. A friend of mine saw the movie in
which…

But he can't bring himself to say it out loud. He leans over and whispers something to Thomas.

22. INTERIOR, WAREHOUSE—DAY

Jan and Kurt drag Edward into a huge abandoned building and toss him against the wall. He slides to the floor, already weak from being beaten. Jan and Kurt step aside to compare notes, perfect corporate functionaries.

                KURT
Kill him now or contact Frankfurt first?

                JAN
Frankfurt?

                KURT
Right?

                JAN
Amsterdam.

                KURT
You sure?

Jan checks his pocket diary.

                JAN
London.

                KURT
             (realizes)
Ah, right.

                JAN
Tie him up.

Kurt does as he's told as Jan moves to the window and flips open his cellular phone. He dials a number and has trouble getting a connection. He tries again but it's the same thing. Kurt finishes tying Edward to a radiator.

JAN
(of phone)
This thing is a piece of shit.

KURT
You should've gotten the one I got.

JAN
Which one is that?

KURT
The DX-2047.

JAN
But that's what this one is.

KURT
No, look, that's a DX-2046. It's outdated.

JAN
It's brand new.

KURT
The technology improves daily.

JAN
How much you pay for that?

KURT
I lease it.

JAN
Really?

KURT
Yeah, works out cheaper in the long run.

Jan puts his phone away and glances over at Edward.

JAN
Get the lamp.

KURT

Right.

Kurt brings him a busted floor lamp that lies near the door. Keeping his eyes on Edward, Jan cuts the cord off at the base of the lamp. He holds up the split wires and sees that the copper at the end of each is exposed. Kurt takes this and plugs the cord into the wall socket, careful to keep the exposed ends away from one another. He comes up behind Edward and holds them inches away from the captive's temples.

EDWARD

Jan, I don't have anything to do with Thomas anymore. I haven't seen him in over a year.

JAN

You know where Sofia is.

Edward is taken off guard by this.

EDWARD
(fakes ignorance)

Sofia?

JAN

The girl. His wife?

EDWARD

No. I don't. I don't know where she is.

Jan nods to Kurt and he brings the two exposed wires to Edward's temples. ZAPPP!!!! Edward jerks violently forward and Kurt steps back. Jan waits.

JAN

Sofia Ludens.

EDWARD
(recovers, gasps)

What do you want with her? She doesn't know anything.

Jan nods to Kurt again and—ZAPPP!!!!!—he shocks Edward just a little bit longer. Stepping back, Kurt sees Edward is trembling violently. He has trouble trying to speak.

>   EDWARD
> Jan, look, we go way back. We were accountants
> together. You were a good accountant.
>
>   JAN
> I was younger then. I didn't know any better.
> I moved up. I'm more realistic now.
>
>   EDWARD
> What if I told you Sofia killed Thomas?
>
>   JAN
> I'd say you were lying.
>
>   EDWARD
> But it's true.
>
>   JAN
> Is it? Well, that's great. That's what we're
> here to find out. But first I've got to know
> where this girl, Sofia, is.
>
>   EDWARD
> I won't tell you anything.
>
>   JAN
> Do you realize we're going to torture you?
>
>   EDWARD
> I won't tell you anything about Sofia.
>
>   JAN
>   *(to Kurt)*
> He's a martyr.
>
>   KURT
> A hopeless romantic.

                    JAN
            Give me your phone.

He takes Kurt's mobile phone, steps away, dials, listens, and has trouble with this one too.

                    JAN
            This is just as bad as mine.

                    KURT
            What?

Kurt takes it, dials, and gets no signal.

                    KURT
            Batteries must be low.

                    JAN
            I'm going down to the street and make some
            calls. See what you can get out of him.

                    KURT
            Right.

Jan leaves. Kurt walks back and lifts the power cord back up off the floor.

                    KURT
            Edward, don't take this personally, okay?

23. EXTERIOR, ISABELLE'S PLACE—DAY

Thomas is waiting for Isabelle on the front steps of her building. She arrives and is clearly depressed.

                    THOMAS
            Hey.

                    ISABELLE
                (checks her mailbox)
            Hello.

THOMAS
What's wrong?

ISABELLE
I'm mediocre.

THOMAS
You are, huh?

ISABELLE
I am. And I'm not sensual.

THOMAS
No, you're definitely sensual.

ISABELLE
I'm coldly intellectual. Too pale. Altogether too ethereal. And my feet hurt from wearing these stupid shoes.

She sits beside him, removes her shoe, and rubs her foot.

THOMAS
You want to make love?

ISABELLE
No. Not now. Not yet. I'm tired and aggravated.

THOMAS
I'd like to rent a movie.

ISABELLE
A dirty movie?

THOMAS
Yeah.

ISABELLE
Okay. This is my membership card for the video store. It's over there by where the white supremacists hang out.

24. EXTERIOR, PIZZERIA—DAY

Jan is talking on the pay phone as Kurt approaches. He covers the receiver.

>   JAN
>   How's it going?
>
>   KURT
>   He's had it.
>
>   JAN
>   Did you get anything out of him?
>
>   KURT
>   *(hands him a slip of paper)*
>   Address downtown. Tribeca. I'm gonna get
>   something to eat.
>
>   JAN
>   Get a receipt.
>
>   KURT
>   Right.

Jan returns to his phone call as Kurt enters the pizza parlor, shoving a customer out of his way at the counter.

25. INTERIOR, WAREHOUSE—DAY

A pair of young squatters, Ted and Nicola, enter the vast space.

>   NICOLA
>   Where is it?
>
>   TED
>   Back here.
>
>   NICOLA
>   *(of river view)*
>   Oh, look at the water!

TED

That's the Hudson. That's New Jersey over there.

NICOLA

No way!

TED

Yeah.

He finds his floor lamp.

NICOLA
(skeptical)
That's it? That's your lamp?

TED

You like it?

NICOLA

It's got no plug.

TED
(sees this, angry)
Hey! What the…

NICOLA
(of their new home)
I like the breeze. You told me New York wasn't gonna be as hot as Georgia.

TED

Someone's tampered with my lamp!

NICOLA
(unfazed, of Edward)
There's a dead man in the corner.

TED
(drops lamp, terrified)
Bullshit.

But she points him out and Ted cautiously approaches.

26. INTERIOR, VIDEO STORE—DAY

Thomas finds the tape he's looking for. A clerk approaches.

> THOMAS
> You work here?

> CLERK
> Yeah.

> THOMAS
> I'd like to rent this tape.

Thomas hands the tape to the clerk.

> CLERK
> Sofia Ludens, huh?

> THOMAS
> You know it?

> CLERK
> You can get arrested for watching this stuff.

> THOMAS
> *(worried)*
> Yeah?

> CLERK
> No.

Irritated, Thomas grabs the box back from the clerk and walks to the next aisle. The clerk follows.

> CLERK
> You're a pretty naïve guy, huh?

> THOMAS
> I've got amnesia.

                    CLERK
            Drag. You a member?

                    THOMAS
            No. But a friend of mine is.

He hands over Isabelle's card.

                    CLERK
                    (reads)
            "Isabelle." Oh yeah, she comes in here all the
            time.

                    THOMAS
            She does, huh?

Thomas walks back to the first aisle, offended somehow.

                    CLERK
                    (apologizes)
            I didn't mean anything by that.

Thomas places the videotape on the counter by the register, eager to leave.

                    THOMAS
            Good. Here. What do I owe you?

27. INTERIOR, WAREHOUSE—DAY

Edward is still alive, barely. Ted and Nicola have dragged him nearer the windows. His head is resting in Nicola's lap, while Ted pours a cap full of whiskey from his hip flask.

                    NICOLA
            We should give him some water, don't you
            think?

                    TED
                    (leans in with cap)
            We don't have any water.

NICOLA
I need to take a shower, Ted.

TED
Lift his head a little.

She does this and Ted carefully pours the whiskey into Edward's gaping mouth. Nothing happens. They watch and wait. Edward remains unconscious.

NICOLA
Give him some more.

Ted complies. This time Edward coughs and lifts his head out of Nicola's lap, startled.

TED
(proud)
See, it works!

NICOLA
(of whiskey)
Gimme some.

TED
It's all we got.

NICOLA
(drinks, looks around)
This place ain't so bad, really.

Edward rolls up off the floor and crouches like an animal in the corner, staring warily at the two young people.

NICOLA
Do you think he's dangerous?

TED
(leads her further away)
Could be. I got my knife ready in case he does anything weird.

                    NICOLA
Maybe he's rabid.

                    TED
Rabid?

                    NICOLA
Yeah, you know, like when somebody has
rabies.

                    TED
Could be. Could be he got bit by a rat.

                    NICOLA
Are there rats in here?

                    TED
Rats with rabies?

                    NICOLA
God, I hope not.

Edward continues to stare at them.

28. EXTERIOR, WAREHOUSE—NIGHT

Later, as the sun goes down, Edward moves shakily away from the warehouse. Ted and Nicola watch him go.

                    NICOLA
                (calls)
Honey, you be careful out there!

                    TED
Oh, Nicola, let him be. He's gotta learn to get
along on his own.

                    NICOLA
I'm worried about him.

She tries to follow Edward but Ted holds her back.

                    TED
Why are you worried about him? Come on,
now. Why are you worried about that man?
We gotta—

                   NICOLA
              (calls to Edward)
Are you gonna be okay?!

                    TED
Come on.

He leads her back inside as Edward stumbles off into the city.

29. INTERIOR, ISABELLE'S PLACE—NIGHT

Thomas watches the videotape he has rented. In the film, Sofia Ludens is involved in an orgy with five or six people. Isabelle is in the bath, reading a book. Hearing the TV, she lowers it and listens closer.

                  ISABELLE
What are you watching?

                   THOMAS
Something called *Gang Rape*.

Baffled, Thomas picks up the remote control and pauses the TV. Isabelle in the doorway appears wearing a robe. She is immediately startled when she sees the paused image of Sofia on the screen. Thomas notices this and watches as she moves slowly towards the TV set and reaches out to touch the image.

                   THOMAS
What is it?

                  ISABELLE
I know this girl.

                   THOMAS
It's Sofia Ludens.

ISABELLE
You know her.

THOMAS
No.

ISABELLE
How do you know her name?

THOMAS
It's written on the box.

ISABELLE
Why did you get this tape?

THOMAS
I was curious about the name Sofia. You said in my sleep I said that name. And then this kid in the park, he—

ISABELLE
You don't recognize her.

THOMAS
No.

Isabelle leans forward and holds her head as if in pain. Concerned, Thomas comes close and lays a hand on her shoulder.

ISABELLE
This is it.

THOMAS
This is what?

ISABELLE
This is the thing I'm supposed to do.

THOMAS
(out of his depth)
Yeah?

ISABELLE
This is it. This is the sign. This girl.

THOMAS
Are you sure? How can you tell?

ISABELLE
I just know. I can see it. It's in her face. And you're part of it.

THOMAS
(scared, falls back)
How can I possibly be part of... of what?

ISABELLE
You have to be. Why else would you have come to me?

THOMAS
I didn't come to you. We met in a coffee shop.

ISABELLE
Yes. That's true. But you've brought me the sign.

He looks at the frozen image of Sofia on the TV and worries.

THOMAS
How do you know it's a sign?

ISABELLE
Because I do.

THOMAS
You could've gotten this sign yourself by going over to the video store.

ISABELLE
Yes. But I didn't. You did.

Thomas is increasingly frightened. As he again looks at the TV,

Isabelle reaches out to touch his hand and reassure him. But he jumps back, afraid of her too.

                THOMAS
    You think God wants you to find this girl?

                ISABELLE
    She's in trouble. I'm certain of it.

                THOMAS
    And what are you going to do about that?

She hesitates, looks from him to the TV, then sits on the bed.

                ISABELLE
    I don't know.

30. INTERIOR, PIZZERIA—NIGHT

Edward comes up the sidewalk with dangerous intensity, a man possessed, his shirttails hanging out, his tie askew, his hair jolted stiff by electrocution. He storms into the pizzeria, terrifying people who scatter and flee. Edward takes what he wants to eat and drink, then strides off on his mission.

31. EXTERIOR, CITY STREET—NIGHT

Thomas and Isabelle come around the corner into a deserted street in Tribeca. He pauses, looking around. She watches him.

                THOMAS
    Where are we now?

                ISABELLE
    The coffee shop is up that way.

                THOMAS
    Sixth Avenue?

                ISABELLE
    Back there.

                    THOMAS
            The water's that way, right?

                    ISABELLE
            Yes. But there's water that way, too.

                    THOMAS
                  (moves on)
            It was a street with cobblestones. I remember
            seeing the blood on the cobblestones.

32. EXTERIOR, ALLEY—NIGHT

They pause in the street at the end of the alley where Thomas first awoke. Isabelle hangs back and watches him as he slowly, gradually drifts towards the exact spot. She follows him till he stops.

                    THOMAS
            This is it.

                    ISABELLE
            Are you sure?

                    THOMAS
            Yes. I remember.

Isabelle kneels and looks at the ground.

                    ISABELLE
            There is glass all over.

Thomas gets down with her and sees shattered glass across the paving stones. Hearing the creaking of a rusty hinge, they look up at the wall of the building beside them and see a large windowed door on the third floor swinging slightly open and shut in the breeze. The glass in the door is busted and the loft space within seems dark.

33. INTERIOR, LOFT—NIGHT

After a little effort to pick the lock, the door opens and Thomas enters cautiously. Isabelle follows. They look, listen, and decide the place is empty. It's a large industrial space only partially renovated into an elegant loft. The contractor's tools and supplies are still lying around.

> THOMAS
> *(hands back her hair pin)*

Here.

> ISABELLE

You did that pretty good.

> THOMAS

What?

> ISABELLE

Picking the lock.

> THOMAS

It was easy.

> ISABELLE

Maybe you're a locksmith.

Thomas approaches the open floor-to-ceiling window and looks out and down into the alley. Isabelle investigates an unmade bed positioned near the back of the space. She comes closer, hesitates, then reaches out and touches the tangled sheets. She then sees an open closet. Inside, she finds women's clothes: lingerie, expensive dresses, shoes. Meanwhile, Thomas rummages through some garbage on a table he finds near the window: an empty cigarette box, matches, a straight-edge razor blade, two floppy disks, and a Polaroid snapshot. He lifts the Polaroid into a shaft of light and winces in disgust.

> THOMAS
> *(quietly)*

Shit!

Troubled, he looks around for Isabelle and finds her seated on the edge of the bed, dressed in the frankly sexy clothes she has found.

Thomas at first doesn't recognize her. Isabelle is uncertain of the effect. He comes to her and kneels beside the bed. He folds his hands on her knee and looks away, hiding his face.

> ISABELLE
>
> What is it?

> THOMAS
>
> Do you hope I don't find out who I am?

> ISABELLE
>
> It doesn't matter to me who you were.

Only now does Thomas turn his face to hers. Leaning forward, he kisses her. Clumsily, she accepts and tries her best to kiss him in return. He guides her back onto the bed and lies beside her.

> ISABELLE
>
> Are you remembering who you are?

> THOMAS
> *(he looks away, troubled)*
> No. I don't remember anything.

> ISABELLE
>
> I'm afraid.

> THOMAS
>
> Of me?

> ISABELLE
>
> I'm afraid I won't know how.

> THOMAS
>
> How to what?

> ISABELLE
>
> Make love.

> THOMAS
>
> Don't worry.

                    ISABELLE
    Maybe I won't like it.

Thomas pauses then kisses her lips lightly.

                    THOMAS
    Do you like that?

                    ISABELLE
    Yes.

He kisses her on the shoulder.

                    THOMAS
    Like that?

                    ISABELLE
    Yes. I like that.

He moves his face down her body and Isabelle sighs deeply.

                    THOMAS
    You like that?

                    ISABELLE
    I like that especially. Keep doing that.

                    THOMAS
    What?

                    ISABELLE
    That.

                    THOMAS
    You mean this?

                    ISABELLE
                (blissfully)
    Ohhhh!!!!

But then she stops and sits up.

                    ISABELLE
    What is that?

                    THOMAS
    What?

                    ISABELLE
    Listen.

There are footsteps outside on the stairs. Presently, the door at the front of the loft opens and Jan and Kurt enter with their guns drawn.

                    JAN
    Go check the bedroom. I'll find the lights.

They fan out into the loft. Kurt finds the bedroom area, looks around and sees nothing. He goes back up front where he finds Jan going through the junk on the table just as Thomas did. He finds the floppy disks and lifts them, satisfied. But then they hear the street door down below creak open as Sofia comes in from the sidewalk, looking back into the street, trying not to be noticed. She starts up the stairs. Up in the loft, Jan ducks into the shadows as Kurt steps behind the door. Isabelle and Thomas, hiding in the bedroom closet, listen. The door opens. Sofia creeps in and is immediately apprehended. Kurt gags her and drags her over to show to Jan.

                    JAN
    Yeah, that's her.

                    KURT
    Should I break her neck?

                    JAN
    No. I want to talk to her first.

34. EXTERIOR, PHONE BOOTH—NIGHT

A harried and poor young mother is on the phone while her two little kids try to set fire to the garbage in the can on the corner.

                    MOTHER
                  (hysterical)
          I swear to God, you'll read about it in the
          newspapers tomorrow, Joey! I swear to God!

Edward strides up and shoves her out of his way, grasping the receiver as the woman gets up off the sidewalk, irate.

                    MOTHER
            What the fuck is your problem, pal!

Edward grabs her pocket book and dumps its contents on the ground, rummaging around for change while she kicks him. The kids get the garbage lit just as a police car pulls up and two cops jump out to deal with all this.

35. INTERIOR, LOFT—NIGHT

Sofia has been lashed to the base of a steel pillar in the center of the front room, seated on the floor, her arms tied behind her. Jan comes over with the floppy disks.

                     JAN
          Sofia, my name's Jan. I work for Mister
          Jacques.

                    SOFIA
                (listlessly, defeated)
          I hate you. I hate Jacques. I hate everybody.

                     JAN
          Of course. It's a rough time to be a human
          being. Here, sit up.

                    SOFIA
          What did you do to Edward?

                     JAN
          Edward's dead.

She weakens even more and hangs her head.

JAN

Let's talk about these floppy disks.

SOFIA

Why did you have to do that? He wasn't a danger to you.

Jan, at a loss, looks to Kurt.

JAN

What's she talking about?

KURT

She's upset about the accountant.

Jan realizes, then returns to Sofia.

JAN

Look, forget about Edward. Now, I want to know about these floppy disks. Where'd you get them?

SOFIA
(sighs, depressed)
From Thomas.

JAN

When?

SOFIA

He had them with him yesterday.

JAN

He's here in New York?

SOFIA
(looks right at Jan)
He's dead too.

JAN

Tell the truth.

SOFIA
That is the truth! I pushed him out that window!

Jan looks to Kurt again. They both look at the window. But Kurt shakes his head, not convinced.

KURT
Makes no sense, Jan.

JAN
Edward said the same thing.

KURT
It would've been in the papers. We would've heard.

Jan considers his options, then looks back at Sofia.

JAN
Sofia, look, you're going to have to tell us everything you know about Thomas.

SOFIA
But what can I tell you?

JAN
Why is he in New York?

SOFIA
But he's *dead*!

JAN
Is this where he lives?

SOFIA
Hey! This is my place! I pay the rent with my own money!

KURT
It's a dump.

SOFIA
(offended)
I was having it fixed up. I bought some furniture, but I ran out of money.

KURT
Typical.

JAN
(annoyed)
Kurt, please.

KURT
(lays off)
Right.

Thomas and Isabelle creep carefully out of the closet, listening as they crouch behind the bed.

JAN
Sofia, who has Thomas been in contact with?

SOFIA
I don't know.

JAN
How long has he been in the States?

SOFIA
Please! I hate him just as much as you do! I don't know anything!

Jan and Kurt sit back and size up the situation.

JAN
What do you think, Kurt?

KURT
We could perform a water torture in the bathroom but that could be noisy. But there are things I can do with a pair of pliers.

                    JAN
          Do you need me for anything?

                    KURT
          No.

                    JAN
          Good. I'll go back to the car and check out
          these disks.

36. INTERIOR, POLICE PRECINCT—NIGHT

The cops handcuff Edward to a metal chair at the side of Officer Melville's desk. She is obviously and immediately heartbroken by this sad man's plight.

                    MELVILLE
          Hi. I'm Officer Melville. But you can call me
          Patsy. They send people to me when they
          have no identification. Sometimes they don't
          even know their own name!
                    (looks aside)
          I find that so incredibly sad.
                    (touches Edward's hand)
          Can you understand me? Can you hear what
          I'm saying?

But he just looks past her and stares at the wall. Melville sighs and looks down at her desk, distraught.

                    MELVILLE
          God, I can't take this job.

                    CABAN
                    (shouts from his desk)
          You gotta toughen yourself up, Melville!

                    MELVILLE
                    (angry)
          What do I have to do, become completely
          insensitive!?

                    CABAN
        Just do your job!

Finally, she looks up at Edward again and sees he is still staring at the wall behind her. She turns and follows his gaze to a Polaroid of Thomas pinned up amongst a collection of lost and missing people. She removes the photo from the wall and shows it to Edward.

                    MELVILLE
        Is this a friend of yours?

Edward shakes his head, "no." Melville studies the photo, considers things, then hazards another guess.

                    MELVILLE
        Did this man... harm you in some way?

Edward nods his head, "yes." Melville sighs again and hangs her head, crying quietly.

37. INTERIOR, LOFT—NIGHT

Kurt removes his jacket and holster, hanging them on a hook on the wall far across the loft. Sofia is still lashed to the pillar.

                    KURT
        Can I ask you a personal question?

                    SOFIA
        Leave me alone.

                    KURT
        Do you resent your position as a woman in
        the motion picture industry? I'm sorry. I find
        you very attractive, and I'm interested in
        commodities.

                    SOFIA
                (raises her face to him)
        What are you talking about?

He finds a pair of pliers on the floor and starts untying her shoe.

> KURT
> Well, a commodity is an article of trade; a product in the purest sense.

> SOFIA
> What has this got to do with me?

> KURT
> You're a product.

> SOFIA
> I am?

> KURT
> You're a commodity. Thomas tendered your body in exchange for money.

> SOFIA
> So, I'm an article of trade?

> KURT
> Yes, a "useful thing," in terms of classic capitalism. I studied economics. I know what I'm talking about.

Meanwhile, unseen and quietly, Thomas and Isabelle search for weapons. They find a power drill and Thomas plugs it in.

> KURT
> *(to Sofia, holding pliers)*
> Now I want you to tell me why Thomas was in New York and who he came to see.

> SOFIA
> *(afraid)*
> He came to see me.

> KURT
> Why would he come to see you?

SOFIA
He wanted me back.

KURT
He wanted you *back*?

SOFIA
I ran away.

KURT
From Thomas?

SOFIA
He loved me.

KURT
And you left him?

SOFIA
Yes.

KURT
Why had you left him?

SOFIA
He scared me!

KURT
But you just told me that he loved you?

SOFIA
I just want to change my life.

KURT
What about Thomas?

SOFIA
He took advantage of me.

KURT
And whose fault is that?

                    SOFIA
          I killed him! I did! I swear!

                    KURT
          I don't believe you.

                    SOFIA
          Please don't hurt me!

He shoves a rag in her mouth.

                    KURT
          Why would you be scared of a man who
          loved you?

WHIRRRR!!!!! Kurt and Sofia look away and see Isabelle across the room gunning the electric drill, drop-dead sexy in high heels, a tiny dress, and wielding a shiny power tool.

                    KURT
               (stands, impressed)
          Wow!

But then he looks over and sees Thomas, far across the room, remove the gun from the shoulder holster. Both armed, Thomas and Isabelle pursue Kurt with their weapons. They corner him and send him falling out the window into the alley below.

38. EXTERIOR, ALLEY—NIGHT

At the car, Jan is about to slip the disks into a laptop when he hears Kurt hit the ground with a thud. He leans out of the car and sees his associate lying there in the alley. He gets out, tosses the computer and disks on the front seat, and approaches Kurt, drawing his gun. Coming down over the body, he sees Kurt is dead and looks up at the window above.

39. INTERIOR, LOFT—NIGHT

Isabelle unties Sofia. Once free, the girl jumps up and backs away from Thomas, terrified. Thomas raises his hands and backs off too, showing he means no harm. But Sofia is not reassured. Isabelle gets between them and reaches out for Sofia's hand.

> ISABELLE
> You must come with us. Quickly.

Sofia finally decides she trusts Isabelle.

> SOFIA
> *(of Thomas)*
> What's wrong with him?

> ISABELLE
> He's forgotten who he is.

They hear the street door down below open and close.

> SOFIA
> This way.

She leads them to a freight elevator at the back of the loft.

40. EXTERIOR, ALLEY—NIGHT

They push out through the freight elevator door and find themselves back in the alley. Jan's car is right there before them. Thomas sees the keys are in the ignition and gets in behind the wheel. Isabelle follows but stops and looks back at Sofia who is reluctant to join them.

> ISABELLE
> It's okay, really. Come.

But Sofia stays where she is.

41. INTERIOR, LOFT—NIGHT

Jan enters, ready for a shootout, but finds Sofia is gone. He discovers the freight elevator and curses himself. Just then he hears the car lurch into gear and drive away down below. He runs to the window and watches them escape.

JAN

Fuck!

But then he sees Sofia's bag on the floor. As he lifts it, her change purse falls out. He lifts this, opens it, and finds the address Edward gave her of the house in Portchester written on a small slip of paper.

42. INTERIOR, CAR—NIGHT

Thomas is driving fast and recklessly.

ISABELLE
(alarmed)
Let me drive.

THOMAS
Why?

ISABELLE
Because you don't know how.

THOMAS
I know how, I just can't remember.

ISABELLE
But it's the same thing.

Unsettled, Thomas glances at Sofia in the backseat. She watches him with unveiled suspicion.

THOMAS
(hesitates)
What's the matter with her?

ISABELLE
She's afraid of you.

THOMAS
(disquieted)
Great.

                    ISABELLE
    Let me drive.

                    THOMAS
    No. Come on. We're just…

                    ISABELLE
    Be careful.

                    SOFIA
    Go north.

Thomas slows down and pulls over. He turns and looks back at her, careful not to scare her any further.

                    THOMAS
    Where?

                    SOFIA
    Portchester.

43. INTERIOR, DINER—NIGHT

Later, Thomas is sitting by himself at the counter. Isabelle and Sofia are in a booth by themselves far across the restaurant. They sit in silence awhile, casting glances at Thomas. Finally, Sofia turns away and lights a cigarette.

                    SOFIA
    You're wearing my stuff.

Isabelle only then remembers her new clothes.

                    ISABELLE
    Sorry.

                    SOFIA
    They look good on you.

                    ISABELLE
    Thanks.

Sofia looks Isabelle over, then back at Thomas.

>   SOFIA
> You're in love with him.

>   ISABELLE
> I only just met him.

>   SOFIA
> Is it true he can't remember who he is?

>   ISABELLE
> He has amnesia.

Sofia smokes and looks away.

>   SOFIA
> I hate him anyway.

Isabelle gets out of the booth and joins Thomas. He is anxious for more information.

>   THOMAS
> What'd she say?

>   ISABELLE
> She's in trouble with those men. And she
> doesn't want to go to the police.

>   THOMAS
> Does she know who I am?

>   ISABELLE
> Yes. But she won't tell me.
>   *(with her hand on his)*
> She said you're a very dangerous man.
>   *(stands)*
> I'll be outside.

He watches Isabelle go, then looks over at Sofia. Sofia watches as he approaches, no longer so scared, but mean. He pauses beside her booth.

            THOMAS
    Do you mind if I sit down?

Sofia looks away. He sighs and sits down at the next booth, behind Sofia's back.

            THOMAS
    Look I can't remember anything.
            (no response)
    I can't imagine what I've done to you. But I
    want you to know whatever it is I can do to
    help you, I will.

She betrays no emotion.

            SOFIA
    This woman, Isabelle, who is she?

            THOMAS
    She helped me out.

            SOFIA
    She doesn't know who you are?

            THOMAS
    No. Neither do I.

            SOFIA
    But I do.

            THOMAS
            (tentatively)
    Will you tell me?

She considers this, then decides and stubs out her cigarette. She stands out of the booth and leaves.

            SOFIA
    No. I won't.

44. EXTERIOR, HOUSE—NIGHT

Thomas, Isabelle, and Sofia drive up and get out of the car.

> THOMAS
> *(to Sofia)*
> You got a key?

> SOFIA
> No.

Thomas moves ahead of them, towards the house, and smashes a window.

> ISABELLE
> He's really good at that kind of thing: breaking into places and so on.

> SOFIA
> Tell me about it.

45. INTERIOR, HOUSE—NIGHT

Thomas finishes checking out the ground floor as Isabelle comes down from the rooms above. Sofia remains at the top of the stairs, keeping her distance from Thomas.

> ISABELLE
> There is only one bed upstairs.

> THOMAS
> You get some sleep. I'll stay up. Give me the gun.

Isabelle hesitates, uncertain, glancing quickly up at Sofia.

> THOMAS
> *(impatient)*
> Give me the gun!

She hesitantly takes out the gun, hands it to Thomas, and climbs the stairs to join Sofia. Thomas watches them enter the upstairs room and hears them lock the door behind themselves. Furious, he walks away.

46. INTERIOR, HOUSE—NIGHT

In the bedroom, Isabelle sits on a chair and looks across at Sofia who is curled up on the bed.

> ISABELLE
> Are you sure you don't want to go to the police?

> SOFIA
> They'll only send me back to Holland and Mister Jacques will have me killed when I get there.

> ISABELLE
> Who is Mister Jacques?

> SOFIA
> It doesn't matter.

> ISABELLE
> I know a place not far from here where you can hide for awhile. You'll be safe.

> SOFIA
> I wish they'd just kill me.

Isabelle comes and sits beside her on the bed. She caresses her.

> ISABELLE
> Don't talk like that.

Sofia looks at Isabelle. She's terrified and childlike in her despair.

> SOFIA
> *(confesses softly)*
> I'm not afraid of dying. I'm afraid of pain.

ISABELLE
No one is going to hurt you.

SOFIA
Yesterday I thought I was so smart. Like I was going to help people and stop bad things from happening. I was going to change things. Change my life.
(turns away and sighs)
I got a man killed.

47. INTERIOR, HOUSE—NIGHT

Thomas is sitting at the table with the gun pointed at his head. Isabelle comes down from upstairs and grabs the gun.

ISABELLE
Don't do that!

THOMAS
It's not loaded.

ISABELLE
I know. I emptied it. But who cares.

She returns it to her handbag.

THOMAS
(angry)
You gave me an unloaded gun to protect ourselves with.

ISABELLE
(ashamed)
I was scared.

THOMAS
You don't trust me at all now, do you?

ISABELLE
I'm sorry.

THOMAS
Did you think I was gonna walk in there and shoot the two of you in your sleep?

ISABELLE
(hesitates, sadly)
She told me you had done things like that before.

Thomas is speechless. He looks away from Isabelle and holds his forehead, eyes closed.

THOMAS
What else did she say?

ISABELLE
She said you were in trouble too.

He joins her at the kitchen table.

THOMAS
In trouble with who?

ISABELLE
Those men back there.

THOMAS
And who are they?

ISABELLE
(wearily)
They work for a highly respectable yet ultimately sinister international corporation with political connections.

THOMAS
(skeptical)
Are you making this up?

ISABELLE
No. It's true.

Thomas stands and paces while Isabelle tries to call up data from the floppy disks.

>   THOMAS
> What do they want with me?

>   ISABELLE
> They want to kill you.

>   THOMAS
> Why?

>   ISABELLE
> Because you know what's on these.

>   THOMAS
>   *(takes one)*
> Yeah? What the fuck are these?

>   ISABELLE
> Floppy disks.

>   THOMAS
> Floppy what?

>   ISABELLE
>   *(busy working)*
> Disks.

>   THOMAS
> But they're square.

>   ISABELLE
>   *(concentrating)*
> Shhh!

>   THOMAS
>   *(adds)*
> And they're not floppy either, they're stiff.

But Thomas stops pacing and stares at Isabelle. She has stopped typing and is studying the computer screen.

THOMAS
What is it?

ISABELLE
Financial information. Dates. Bank accounts. Deposits. Withdrawals.

She closes the laptop and sighs. She stands and falls against him for comfort.

ISABELLE
This is it. Whatever it is I'm supposed to do, this is it.

Thomas holds her close, then lets her go and sits down on the stairs.

THOMAS
Isabelle, I don't think this is divine intervention.

ISABELLE
You don't?

THOMAS
No. It's not a miracle. And it's not God's will. You know what I think this is? This, I think, is just really bad luck. And it's got nothing to do with you.
(as she sits beside him)
So, you shouldn't get any more involved than you already are.

ISABELLE
(insists)
I know I was meant to find this girl and to help her.

THOMAS
You do, huh?

ISABELLE
Yes. I think maybe I'm supposed to save her from you.

THOMAS
I'm the same man you knew yesterday.

ISABELLE
(takes his hand, kisses it)
Maybe.

48. INTERIOR, POLICE PRECINCT—DAY

Early morning. Edward is now handcuffed to a heavy bench in the hallway. Officer Melville joins him.

MELVILLE
We have no information on this man. He has no record. We've checked everything.

Edward throws his head back and growls, frustrated. He tugs at his handcuffs. Melville looks on, crushed with pity. Detective Caban passes by and looks Edward up and down, disgusted.

CABAN
This guy's a maniac, Melville.

MELVILLE
(indignant)
Sir, he's troubled.

CABAN
He say anything yet?

MELVILLE
No, nothing.

CABAN
(walks away)
Then get him outta here, Melville. He's a mental case. Not our job.

                    MELVILLE
                  (toughens up)
              I'm sorry. I have to book you. But you get to
              make a phone call.

49. INTERIOR, HOUSE—DAY

The phone rings and Thomas wakes up from where he is sleeping on the floor. It keeps ringing and he hesitates, but then gets up and answers it.

                    THOMAS
                  (careful)
              Hello?

50. INTERIOR, POLICE PRECINCT—DAY

Edward looks at the receiver, recognizing the voice, and hangs up quick.

51. INTERIOR, HOUSE—DAY

Thomas replaces the receiver, spooked. He sees Sofia still sound asleep in the next room. But Isabelle is nowhere to be seen.

52. INTERIOR, HOSPITAL—DAY

Edward sits in a long hallway, brooding with other unfortunate and homeless misfits. There is one armed guard at the entrance. Melville signs some forms and indicates Edward, who watches her without moving. She comes over and undoes his handcuffs.

                    MELVILLE
                  (gentle)
              Don't worry. Everything's going to be alright.

Edward grabs her by the neck and drags her to the ground. People start screaming and diving for cover as he grabs her gun. The guard comes running, drawing his own gun, but Edward fires and the guard goes down. With the gun at her head, Edward drags Melville towards the door.

53. EXTERIOR, HOSPITAL—DAY

Edward runs in front of a car and forces the driver out at gunpoint. He shoves Officer Melville away, jumps in the car, and speeds off.

54. EXTERIOR, TRAIN STATION—DAY

Isabelle is in a phone booth as a train pulls into the station above. She is holding the floppy disks and an addressed envelope. Her call is answered.

> **ISABELLE**
> *(into phone)*
> Yes. George? I know it's early, but I have something interesting. No. It's not disgusting actually, but very damaging documentation of high-level government corruption. I don't know what government exactly. Maybe a few.

Meanwhile, Jan steps down from the train platform and sees his car parked by the curb. He looks around, sees Isabelle, but doesn't know her. He stands aside and waits to see if she approaches the car.

> **ISABELLE**
> Okay. Look, George, I'm on the run from a group of bloodthirsty corporate assassins and I'm hiding in the country. Okay. I'll call you when I can. Expect an envelope tomorrow. Bye.

She hangs up, steps out of the booth, seals the envelope, and drops it into a mailbox. Then she approaches the car. Just as she is about to open the door, Jan rushes in and grabs her by the wrist, holding his gun to the small of her back.

55. INTERIOR, HOUSE—DAY

Sofia wakes. She lies there a moment, then rolls over and sees Thomas at the window, looking out into the yard. She dares not move. Thomas turns back into the room and finds her awake.

>   THOMAS
>   Where's Isabelle?

>   SOFIA
>   I don't know.

>   THOMAS
>   The car is gone.

She just stares at him, afraid. He shakes his head, frustrated.

>   THOMAS
>   Look, I'm not going to hurt you. Relax.

She slides off the bed, sits in the chair, and starts putting on and lacing up her boots. The phone rings again. He looks from it to Sofia. She looks off at it as well, then to Thomas.

>   THOMAS
>   It rang before too.

>   SOFIA
>   Did you answer it?

>   THOMAS
>   Well, yes.

The phone keeps ringing.

>   SOFIA
>   *(rolls her eyes)*
>   Why?

>   THOMAS
>   I thought it might be Isabelle.

>   SOFIA
>   You idiot! They probably know where we
>   are now!

THOMAS
Well, how was I supposed to know?

SOFIA
(in disbelief)
How were you supposed to know? You used to know everything!

THOMAS
(defensive)
Oh yeah? Well, then why don't you tell me about what I used to know!

SOFIA
Why don't you just go and answer the phone!

THOMAS
Fuck you!

SOFIA
Drop dead!

THOMAS
Listen, you! I've had about enough of this shit! Are you gonna tell me who I am and what's going on around here or what!

The phone keeps ringing.

SOFIA
(spiteful)
You want to know who you are?

THOMAS
Yes!

SOFIA
Why should I tell you who you are?

THOMAS
Because I'm asking you to!

                    SOFIA
And I'm supposed to do whatever you want
me to do, is that it?

                    THOMAS
Forget it! I don't care! I don't want to know!

                    SOFIA
Now, you see, that's just like you!

                    THOMAS
What is?!

She looks away, victorious.

                    SOFIA
Answer the phone!

                    THOMAS
You answer the goddamn phone!

And he storms down the stairs. Sofia, left there alone, listens as the phone rings and rings and rings. Finally, she goes out to the landing at the top of the stairs, hesitates, and answers it.

                    SOFIA
                (cautious)
Hello?

                    JAN
                (off)
Sofia, it's Jan.

Her mouth falls open and she'd scream if she could, but she's too scared.

                    JAN
I've got Isabelle and I know where you are.
Now, I'm going to make you a deal. You tell
me if Thomas is with you; just answer yes
and you and Isabelle won't be harmed. But

if you say no, Isabelle is dead.

She nearly faints.

>   JAN
> Yes, or no. Is he with you? If he is, there'll
> be a knock at the door in five minutes. Let
> him answer it. Yes or no? Yes: and you and
> Isabelle are free. No: and Isabelle is dead.

She looks down to Thomas standing at the bottom of the stairs watching her, concerned.

>   JAN
> Sofia, yes or no?

She looks away from Thomas, finally, and stares at the wall.

>   SOFIA
>   *(into phone)*
> Yes.

Jan hangs up. Sofia slowly lowers the receiver but still holds onto it. She glances back down the stairs at Thomas who takes a step closer.

>   THOMAS
> Are you okay?

And she passes out, collapsing there on the landing, still holding the phone. Thomas bounds up the stairs to help her but stops when he hears a car pull up outside. Uncertain what to do, he lifts Sofia off the floor and carries her into the bedroom just as the front door is kicked in. It's Edward. He stalks through the ground floor rooms with his stolen gun. Finding nothing, he starts up the stairs. He finds Sofia in bed, asleep, then prowls around the upstairs rooms, looking for Thomas. Thomas is hiding in the bathroom, panicked. He looks around for a weapon and finds a rusty old razorblade. Finally, Edward roams back into the bedroom. Sofia wakes and sees him. She sits up, about to speak, but Edward raises a finger to his lips, signaling her to keep quiet. As Edward steps back into the hallway, Thomas steps up behind him and holds the razorblade to his throat just as Edward puts the gun to Thomas's head. They remain there, close and still, neither one able or willing to move, as Sofia emerges quietly from the bedroom and out onto the landing again.

                    SOFIA
        Oh, Edward! You're alive!

But Jan appears in the open door at the foot of the stairs, takes aim, and shoots Sofia. Edward swings around, shoots, and catches Jan in the chest, throwing him back out of the house. Now Isabelle stumbles in. Thomas falls down over Sofia to see if she's breathing as Edward runs down the stairs, past Isabelle, and out of the house.

56. EXTERIOR, HOUSE—DAY

Edward runs out of the house and shoots Jan repeatedly as he tries to reach the road. The assassin continues stumbling along until Edward uses up all his ammunition. Finally, he collapses face down in the grass.

57. EXTERIOR, HOUSE—DAY

Moments later, Thomas carries Sofia to the car. Isabelle guides Edward, who is completely disoriented and helpless. She forces him into the car and helps Thomas with Sofia.

                    THOMAS
        Let me drive.

                    ISABELLE
        No. I know the way.

She gets in behind the wheel herself.

58. EXTERIOR, HOUSE—DAY

Half an hour later, Detective Caban finishes taking a look at Jan's body, then indicates that it should be taken away. A younger detective, Olsen, steps up holding Officer Melville's gun in a plastic bag.

> OLSEN
> It is Melville's gun, sir.

> CABAN
> Have we got a trace on the car?

> OLSEN
> It's been spotted. There's an officer in pursuit.

> CABAN
> Where?

> OLSEN
> About five miles away, headed east, toward the river.

> CABAN
> Anything in that direction?

> OLSEN
> Yes, sir. A convent.

59. EXTERIOR, CONVENT—DAY

Isabelle knocks on the front door of the convent and waits. She glances back at her friends: Thomas still carrying the bleeding Sofia, the madman Edward. Then a nun, Sister Amelia, opens the door and looks out at them all, alarmed.

> AMELIA
> *(incredulous)*
> Isabelle?

Isabelle meekly lowers her head and waits to be admitted.

60. INTERIOR, CONVENT—DAY

The doors open and they all rush in, met by a few more nuns who lead them to the infirmary. Thomas sets Sofia down and the nuns take over. The mother superior, Sister Celestine, shoves Thomas out of the way and examines the wounds. She sighs grumpily.

CELESTINE
This is bad.
(to Isabelle, of Thomas)
Who's he?

ISABELLE
He's my friend.

CELESTINE
Tell him to wait outside.

Not needing to be told, Thomas moves off with attitude. Celestine looks at Isabelle's highly sexualized attire.

CELESTINE
(continues)
Isabelle, are you in trouble?

ISABELLE
(nods)
Yes.

Celestine prepares for her work on Sofia's wounds.

CELESTINE
I knew you'd get into trouble. I knew it.
You should never have left here! Never!

Sofia regains consciousness and reaches up to touch Isabelle's arm. Isabelle leans closer as the wounded girl attempts to speak, her voice weak and hesitant.

SOFIA
Let me... tell you. Let me tell you who he is.

Isabelle looks self-consciously to Celestine. Seeing they need privacy, the older nun steps outside.

61. EXTERIOR, CONVENT CLOISTER—DAY

Thomas sits on a bench opposite Edward who presses himself back against the far wall—as far away from Thomas as possible. Celestine arrives.

> THOMAS
> *(stands, anxious)*
> How is she?

> CELESTINE
> The bullet shattered her shoulder bone. We can stop the bleeding, but you've got to get her to a hospital.
> *(of Edward)*
> Now what's his problem?

Thomas looks back at Edward and shrugs; he honestly doesn't know.

> CELESTINE
> *(heads back inside)*
> The girl wants to talk to you.

62. INTERIOR, CONVENT—DAY

Thomas enters and has to lean down over Sofia as she works to raise her voice to a faint whisper.

> SOFIA
> I told her. I told Isabelle. I told her everything. I told her who you are. I can't forgive you. I can only forget. And I don't want to.

She breathes deeply and closes her eyes. He watches her drift off to sleep again.

63. EXTERIOR, CONVENT CLOISTER—DAY

Stupefied, Thomas wanders out and finds Isabelle sitting in the doorway that leads out to a garden. She's been crying. Thomas touches her shoulder and she flinches. Hurt and saddened, he takes his hand away.

THOMAS
I'm sorry.

ISABELLE
But what are you sorry for? Do you know?

He steps aside and sits away from her, with his back to her, in another doorway leading into another garden.

THOMAS
No. I don't. I don't know what I'm sorry for.
But I am sorry. That's got to mean something,
right? I mean, whatever it is she told you,
whatever it is I was—this is me, now. What
else can I do?

Isabelle waits, then stands and crosses to him. She kneels and leans her forehead against his back.

ISABELLE
Will you still make love to me?

He stands slowly and turns to her. He guides her to her feet and they kiss. Then—

THOMAS
Eventually.

She smiles sadly and he feels better.

THOMAS
I'll go get the car.

ISABELLE
Wait. Here. Take the gun. I've put the bullets
back in.

He looks from her to the gun, smiles, then kisses her once again.

He takes the weapon and walks away. She watches him go, then sits, drying the tears from her eyes. Suddenly, she looks up, hearing a scrape and scuffle off to her left and sees a sharpshooter policeman creeping through the foliage just outside the convent wall. Isabelle starts running after Thomas, who is striding up the main hall towards the front door.

                    ISABELLE
    Thomas!

Thomas, gun in hand, pulls back the bolt from the huge front door and looks back over his shoulder as he thinks he hears Isabelle calling.

                    ISABELLE
    Thomas!

As he turns away, the huge doors swing slowly open, revealing an army of police poised to shoot. Thomas whips back around with his gun drawn and is shot through the heart. Hearing the shot from within the convent, Isabelle stops short and shivers. Outside, Detective Caban rolls Thomas over and looks.

                    CABAN
    This isn't him.

Caban, Olsen, and the assembled policemen step aside as Isabelle appears. She comes down over Thomas.

                    CABAN
    Miss? Excuse me, miss. Do you know this man?

Isabelle doesn't respond immediately. She searches Thomas's face, touches his lips, and slowly lifts her eyes to the detective and the others.

                    ISABELLE
    Yes. I know this man.

~The End

Flirt

01. INTERIOR, EMILY'S APARTMENT—DAY

Bill and Emily have been making love all afternoon. Still laying in bed, they discuss their future.

> EMILY
> I feel disgusting.

> BILL
> Why?

> EMILY
> I'm a liar.

> BILL
> No, you're not.

> EMILY
> He writes to me and says he misses me. He calls me and says he loves me. And I reply, "I miss you too."
> *(adds, to Bill)*
> But I don't.

> BILL
> Maybe you don't know what you feel.

> EMILY
> But I *do* know what I feel. I love you. Maybe I love him too. But I definitely love you more.

> BILL
> And I love you.

She sighs and gets off the bed, wrapping a sheet around herself.

> EMILY
> We're using the same language I use when I lie to him.

Bill steps out of bed and pulls on his trousers.

BILL
What time's your flight?

EMILY
Seven o'clock.

BILL
He's going to meet you at the airport in Paris?

EMILY
Yes.

BILL
What will you tell him?

EMILY
(forthright)
What do you want me to tell him?

BILL
(evasive)
I don't want to tell you what to do.

EMILY
Then tell me what you want.

BILL
That would be the same thing.

EMILY
(losing patience)
It would help me decide.

BILL
He wants you to stay with him in Paris?

EMILY
Yes.

BILL
He wants to marry you?

EMILY

I guess. Eventually.

BILL

What do you want me to say?

EMILY

I want you to tell me if there is a future for me and you.

BILL
(now he's worried)
A future, huh?

EMILY

Yes.

BILL

How can I answer that?

EMILY

Yes or no.

BILL

I can't see the future.

EMILY

You don't need to see it if you know it's there.

BILL

What time's your flight?

EMILY

Seven.

BILL
(checks his wristwatch)
Seven, huh? Okay. It's four now. Look, let me go get Michael's truck. I'll drive you to the airport.

                    EMILY
          I can take a taxi.

Bill comes to her and takes her hands.

                    BILL
          No. I want to. Can you wait here?

                    EMILY
                  (carefully)
          How long?

                    BILL
          An hour and a half.

                    EMILY
          And then what?

                    BILL
          I'll tell you the future.

                    EMILY
                  (skeptical)
          At five-thirty?

                    BILL
          Without fail.

She studies his face and decides to believe him.

                    EMILY
          Okay. Five-thirty.

They kiss.

02. EXTERIOR, STREET—DAY

Bill throws on his coat as he makes his way up the sidewalk. A title card announces: New York, 1993. He locates a pay phone. But it's occupied. He waits until an attractive girl finishes her call. She's aggravated.

                    GIRL
                (into phone)
    No.
    No.
    No.
                (then, surprised)
    No?

She and Bill make eye contact. She smiles apologetically. He gestures and indicates she shouldn't hurry. Then she's called back to her conversation.

                    GIRL
                (continues into phone)
    My time is up. I'll call you right back.

She hangs up and searches in her purse for a quarter. Not finding one, she smiles again at Bill.

                    GIRL
    Excuse me, have you got a quarter?

                    BILL
    Sure.

He finds some change in his pocket and hands her a quarter. Their hands touch and linger. She smiles coquettishly and drifts back to the receiver. Bill stands aside and looks around, furtively assessing the girl's figure, impressed. She dials and continues her conversation.

                    GIRL
                (into phone)
    It's me again.
    No.
    No?
    No, no!
                (relaxes, concedes)
    No.

Her gaze drifts back to Bill and when he gestures that he'll just move along, she reaches out and urges him to stay. Finally—

> GIRL
> *(continues into phone)*
> Okay. Yeah. Bye.
> *(hangs up, to Bill)*
> Sorry.

> BILL
> Don't worry about it.

> GIRL
> Thank you.

> BILL
> See you around.

> GIRL
> Maybe.

And she moves off. Bill watches her go as he steps into the booth and dials. Finally, getting an answer, he forgets all about the girl.

> BILL
> *(into phone)*
> Margaret? It's me, Bill. It's important. I need to ask you one question. I want you to tell me if there is a future for me and you.
> *(waits, listens, then)*
> Yes or no.
> *(listens again, then)*
> You don't need to see it if you know it's there. Look, meet me at the bar in ten minutes.

03. INTERIOR, BAR—DAY

Bill enters and approaches the bartender, Mac.

> MAC
> *(resolute)*
> You owe me money.

BILL
(ignores this)
Margaret been in?

MAC
No.

BILL
Let me get a beer, will ya?

MAC
You *do* owe me money.

BILL
I owe lots of people money.

Mac gets him a beer and Bill pays. Towards the back of the room, he finds his friend Michael reading aloud from a book.

MICHAEL
(reading, impressed)
"But such hours of worldly delight were followed by others of deepest despondency in which he considered himself eternally damned."

BILL
Let me borrow your truck. I gotta drive Emily to the airport.

MICHAEL
She's finally leaving you, huh?

BILL
(irritated)
Hey, look, she's just going away to France because she's got a job there for three months, okay?

MICHAEL
You hear the news?

BILL
What news?

MICHAEL
Margaret left her husband.

Bill sets down his beer and comes closer, excited and alarmed.

BILL
You know that for a fact?

MICHAEL
Well, I guess so. I got it from Trish.

Bill tries to keep calm, pauses, and confesses—

BILL
Michael, something happened between me and Margaret.

MICHAEL
Yeah? Like what?

BILL
We got romantic.

MICHAEL
Excuse me?

BILL
Romantic.

MICHAEL
(tries to imagine)
Romantic?

BILL
We kissed. Once.

MICHAEL
Ah! Romantic!

BILL
Yeah.

MICHAEL
When?

BILL
A few weeks ago.

MICHAEL
How?

Bill stands and paces, mentally reconstructing the episode.

BILL
We were at a party. She and Walter had had a fight. She was upset. I got her a drink. She cried on my shoulder. I told her a joke.
(stops and looks at Michael)
We kissed.

MICHAEL
But what about Emily?

BILL
Emily all of a sudden wants me to tell her the future.

MICHAEL
Emily's a pretty remarkable girl.

BILL
Yeah, but Margaret has always fascinated me too.

MICHAEL
(thinks, then)
I'd go for the sure thing.

BILL
You would, huh?

MICHAEL
Emily loves you—you love her.

BILL
Yeah, but she's going away to France for three months.

MICHAEL
Well, don't you trust her?

BILL
Yeah, but I'm already the guy she's seeing behind her boyfriend's back.

MICHAEL
(understands)
That's complicated. But then Margaret is married to Walter.

BILL
But she just left him.

MICHAEL
That's true.

BILL
They could get back together again, though.

MICHAEL
Happens all the time.

BILL
Unless I get in there now and make my play.

MICHAEL
Might be your only chance to know for sure.

04. INTERIOR, BAR KITCHEN—DAY

Trish is one of the waitresses. She's impatient, but Bill demands a moment of her time.

TRISH
Look, Bill, Margaret's in a very mixed-up place in her life right now. She doesn't need to get mixed up with someone like you.

BILL
Someone like me? What's that supposed to mean?

TRISH
You know what I mean.

BILL
No, I don't.

TRISH
You're not serious.

BILL
Serious like Walter, you mean?

TRISH
Hey! Walter's a pretty successful and well thought of guy most of the time!

BILL
He's smothering her.

TRISH
Well, that's no reason for her to take up with an aimless flirt like you.

BILL
Hey!

TRISH
You are with a different girl every time I see you.

BILL
So, I'm lucky!

                TRISH
You're not lucky, Bill. You're loose. You
just can't careen around from one cute little
behind to the next, never investing anything
in any one of them.

                BILL
What about Emily?

                TRISH
What *about* Emily?

                BILL
I've been with Emily for six months and I
haven't strayed once.

                TRISH
So, what do you want, a medal!

She turns away, angry and frustrated. Bill gives his cigarettes to the teenage dishwasher who is sitting there on his break, hearing all this.

                BILL
Here, go smoke my cigarettes.

The dishwasher takes the cigarettes and leaves. Bill approaches Trish.

                BILL
What? Are you upset?

She turns back and considers him carefully, sadly, then embraces him. They kiss. Then—

                TRISH
Your problems are trivial.

05. INTERIOR, BAR MEN'S ROOM—DAY

Moment's later, Bill practically collapses into the men's room and hangs his head over the sink. Three men of varying ages and condition pause and look on. Bill stands back and addresses them.

> BILL
> Gentlemen, excuse me. My girlfriend of six months is going away to Paris, France, for three months. She's beautiful, young, intelligent, and very conscientious. She says she loves me and that she'll miss me terribly.
> *(pauses, loosens his collar)*
> She's also got this ex-boyfriend in Paris. He's smart, talented, successful, and he's a real nice guy. Before she leaves, she wants me to tell her if there's a future for us—for me and for her.
> *(washes his hands at sink)*
> My question is this: am I wrong in wanting more time? More proof. Is it wrong of me to be so scared?

He steps back from the sink, dries his hands, and waits for a reply. One of the men, a professional of some sort in a suit and tie, finishes pissing at the urinal, zips up, and considers the question carefully.

> FIRST MAN
> It's important to keep the girl constantly within your sphere of influence. Of course, this is difficult to do if she is in another country. I would not feel guilty about this fear of losing her. People are people and things happen. But perhaps the things that do happen are not serious. I would write many letters, daily if possible. And I do not think it inadvisable to let her know, frankly and before she leaves, that you have these fears of losing her. She's young, perhaps she's impressionable. This sounds harsh and manipulating, I know. But remember: she's not just going anywhere. She's going to Paris, France.

A workman of some sort is seated on the toilet in the stall with the door half open, preoccupied with his newspaper.

> SECOND MAN
> Relinquishing our hold on someone is an act
> of love. The giving of affection and the
> determination to provide comfort are the two
> practicable elements of love.
> *(sets paper aside)*
> Love requires no proof. Seen in this light,
> love is a sort of faith, since a faith that
> required proof wouldn't be a faith at all. But
> I will make this distinction: love is an act and
> faith is an ability.

The third man is older and down on his luck, unshaven and distracted, looking out through a small dirty window into the alley.

> THIRD MAN
> The best of all possible approaches to this
> dilemma is for the two of you to firmly
> embrace reality for what it is: cruel, brutal,
> cold, and totally unconcerned with the
> individual.

Back in the toilet stall, the second man leans forward and glances out at this sad man at the window. Settling back, he retrieves his newspaper and continues reading.

> SECOND MAN
> *(sighs)*
> I don't want to sound despairing or at a loss
> for ideas, but the fact is you can do nothing
> to retain this girl's love but be the best man
> you know how to be.

06. INTERIOR, BAR—DAY

Meanwhile, Margaret's agitated husband, Walter, enters from the street and comes to the bar. He sets down a handgun and a box of bullets before reaching for his wallet.

                    MAC
               (worried)
          Hey, Walter.

                    WALTER
          Bill been in here today?

                    MAC
          He's in the men's room.

                    WALTER
          Gimme a bottle of Jack Daniels and two
          glasses, Mac. Thank you.

Though concerned, Mac does as he's told. Walter tosses some large denomination bills on the bar. He grabs the bottle, the two glasses, his gun, and his ammunition and sits at a table in back. Bill comes out from the men's room and finds Walter waiting for him. He glances off at Mac and Michael. Mac slowly moves for the phone, but Bill gestures that it's okay. He approaches Walter.

                    BILL
          Evening, Walter.

Walter places a single bullet in the gun and lies the weapon on the table.

                    WALTER
               (without looking up)
          How are you, Bill?

                    BILL
          Mind if I sit down?

                    WALTER
               (with attitude)
          No. Why should *I* mind?

                    BILL
               (sits, of gun)
          What are you gonna do with that?

WALTER
I'm gonna shoot myself.

Bill lifts the gun and removes the bullet.

BILL
That's pretty stupid, Walter.

WALTER
Yeah. I guess I oughta shoot Margaret, huh?

Bill pockets the bullet and lays the gun back down.

BILL
No. You're not gonna shoot anyone.

WALTER
(pours two drinks)
Maybe I oughta shoot you.

BILL
Why me?

WALTER
Because you're a single guy with no responsibilities.
(drinks, pauses, then)
Why is she doing this to me?

BILL
I don't know, Walter.

Walter places another bullet in the gun and places it back down between them.

WALTER
She loved me once. Why can't she love me now?

BILL
People change.

And Bill lifts the gun again, removes the bullet, and places the weapon back on the table.

> WALTER
> I don't change. I don't want to change.

> BILL
> Sometimes you have no choice.

> WALTER
> Have you changed?

> BILL
> I'm changing all the time.

> WALTER
> That's why all the girls like you so much.

> BILL
> The girls don't all like me so much.

> WALTER
> Margaret likes you.

> BILL
> *(eager, encouraged)*
> Did she say that?

Walter glares at him and Bill sits back, hides behind his whiskey, and curses himself for being so stupid.

> BILL
> *(continues)*
> Look, Walter, nothing happened with Margaret and me.

> WALTER
> But it might.

> BILL
> Impossible.

WALTER
(insulted)
Why, don't you think she's attractive?

BILL
(reassures him)
She's *very* attractive.

WALTER
Listen, she's my *wife*, goddamn it!

Bill glances over to Mac and Michael and, again, gestures to them to stay calm. Walter, meanwhile, is reloading the gun.

WALTER
(continues)
Why is it impossible? Why's nothing gonna happen between you and Margaret?

BILL
(thinks, then decides)
Because I'm in love with Emily.

WALTER
(places down loaded gun)
Liar.

BILL
(hurt)
Hey!

WALTER
You've never loved anybody in your life. You go through women like pairs of dirty underwear. You wouldn't know what commitment was if it came up and bit you in the leg!

Genuinely insulted, Bill stands and starts to leave.

BILL
I don't have to sit here and listen to this.

WALTER

Yes, you do.

BILL

I gotta take Emily to the airport.

Walter calms down and nudges Bill's whiskey.

WALTER
(apologizing)
Have a drink.

Bill acquiesces and sits back down. They drink in silence. The guys at the bar look on and hope for the best.

WALTER
(continues)
You ever think of settling down, Bill?

BILL

Occasionally.

WALTER

Lately?

BILL

A little.

WALTER

With Emily?

BILL

Probably.

WALTER

She's a good woman.

Bill considers this seriously and nods.

BILL

Yes, she is.

WALTER
You oughta propose to her.

BILL
(intrigued)
You think so?

WALTER
Yeah.

BILL
Yeah, I guess you're right.

WALTER
You oughta do it now.

Bill pauses with his whiskey raised to his lips.

BILL
Excuse me?

Walter lifts the loaded gun and points it at Bill's head.

WALTER
Call her on the phone. Come on.

Now, Mac and Michael and a few other patrons all duck down behind the bar, some scrambling out the door and fleeing. Walter leads Bill to the phone booth and hands him a quarter.

WALTER
(continues)
Dial.

BILL
Will somebody do something! He's gotta gun, for cryin' out loud!

WALTER
Don't anyone move! I'll shoot him! I swear to God, I'll shoot him! Dial.

Bill feeds the quarter into the pay phone and dials Emily's number. He waits. Finally—

                    BILL
    It's busy.

He hands the receiver to Walter who listens and confirms the line is busy. He hangs up.

                    WALTER
    Damn it!

Just as they're about to return to the table, the phone rings. They both stop and look at it, threatened. Walter stands behind Bill, as if for protection.

                    WALTER
    Answer it.

Bill hesitates, but then goes back and answers.

                    BILL
                (into phone)
    Hello.
                (relieved, he looks to Walter)
    It's Margaret!

Walter suddenly looks terrified and expectant, helpless. Bill sees this and lifts the receiver again.

                    BILL
                (continues, into phone)
    What? No. No. Don't worry about that. No.
    Really. Hey, listen, Walter's here. You wanna
    talk to him?

Walter looks on hopefully. But, reluctantly—

                    BILL
                (continues, into phone)
    No?

Stunned, Walter holds the gun flat against his chest, trying to catch his breath. Bill hangs up and comes to him, placing a hand on the man's shoulder. He's surprised when Walter falls forward, leans his head on Bill's shoulder and cries. The guys at the bar look away in embarrassment. Bill sighs and holds Walter in his arms. But then—POW!—the gun goes off and Bill falls back, holding his face, knocking over some tables and landing on the floor. Walter collapses in a chair. Michael comes down over Bill and looks.

> MICHAEL
> He shot him in the face!

> MAC
> Get your truck! Quick! We gotta get him to a hospital!

Walter stands and tries to say something meaningful but Mac shoves him back down in his chair. He, Michael, and some others carry Bill outside. Walter sits and hangs his head, alone and forgotten, in the empty bar.

07. INTERIOR, HOSPITAL OPERATING ROOM—DAY

Bill is in triage. A female surgeon, Doctor Clint, leans over him and inspects his wounds. A nurse is holding Bill's head still.

> CLINT
> Hmmm. This is bad.
> *(to nurse)*
> Can you wipe all this away?

The nurse cleans up a portion of Bill's face as Clint prepares her instruments. The surgeon turns back and pauses before getting down to business.

> CLINT
> Now, we're going to have to give you something for the pain, but this is going to be painful in any event. Are you allergic to Novocaine?

BILL

No.

She approaches with a needle, trying to decide how to proceed.

CLINT

Okay. Your entire lip is in three pieces. Can you feel that?

BILL

I think so.

CLINT

There are two tears. One goes right across the left cheek. You can feel that, can't you?

BILL

Yes.

CLINT

Are you having any trouble breathing?

BILL

No.

CLINT

Good. Now, I'm going to have to inject the Novocaine directly into the wounds.

BILL

Okay.

CLINT

I'm telling you this because it won't help to ignore what's going on here. I'm going to need you to cooperate.

BILL

Right.

Bill is scared but game, staring up into the blinding white light, the nurse holding his head in place. Her face is beside his, her lips close to his ear.

                        CLINT
                      (meanwhile)
          This is going to pinch a little. There will be a
          number of injections.

She carefully injects the Novocaine and Bill's limbs stiffen, his fingers tightening on the edge of the table.

                        CLINT
                      (continues)
          I know. I know.

                        NURSE
                      (whispers)
          Breathe.

                        CLINT
          One more on this side.

                        NURSE
          Just remember to breathe.

Clint leans away, frustrated.

                        CLINT
          This isn't going to last too long. It's running
          right out of you. There's no place for the
          Novocaine to stay. That's what's in your
          mouth right now, Novocaine, not blood.
          Do you need to spit?

Bill turns and drools into a wad of gauze the nurse holds up to his face.

                        NURSE
                      (soothingly)
          Keep thinking about something. Something
          specific.

BILL
(with effort)
I'm trying.

NURSE
Good. What are you thinking about?

BILL
Girls.

NURSE
That's good. Tell me about the girls.

As Clint busies herself stitching the lip back together, Bill struggles patiently to oblige the nurse.

BILL
Soft... skin... My hand... cupping... her breast. Caressing her... bottom. Her thighs squeezing my... leg. Owww!
(breathes, calms himself, concentrates)
Kissing. Her tongue in... my... mouth. My mouth... on... her breast... spooning...

The nurse is looking dreamily off, lost in his evocation.

NURSE
(curious)
Spooning?

BILL
We lie... side by... side. Your back to me. I put my... arm around your... waist. We draw... up... our knees...

But once again he convulses in pain and can't go on. The nurse snaps out of her revery and focuses on the injured patient.

NURSE
Keep still.

08. INTERIOR, HOSPITAL HALLWAY—NIGHT

Hours later, Bill comes out into the reception area, all bandaged up and with no one there to meet him.

09. EXTERIOR, SIDEWALK PAY PHONE—NIGHT

He listens as the number he's dialed just rings and rings. Finally, he just hangs up and stands there in the cold. But then he sees an available cab approaching and waves it down. The driver stops and Bill steps off the curb, opens the door, and leans down to address him.

>   BILL
> Hey.
>
>   DRIVER
> What happened to you?!
>
>   BILL
> I was shot by the husband of a woman I thought
> I might be in love with. Can you take me to
> a bank machine and then out to the airport?
>
>   DRIVER
> You gonna travel looking like that?
>
>   BILL
> What's wrong with the way I look?

The driver, politely avoiding the obvious facial wound, replies:

>   DRIVER
> You got blood all over your shirt, man.
>
>   BILL
>   *(sits into cab)*
> Come on, let's go.
>
>   DRIVER
> Where to?

> BILL

Paris!

Cut to black.

A title card announces: Berlin, 1994

10. INTERIOR, JOHAN'S APARTMENT—DAY

Dwight is a young Black American man, an out-of-work fashion model, idly flipping through magazines while electronic dance music plays loudly over the sound system.

> JOHAN
> *(off, in German)*
> I feel disgusting.

> DWIGHT

What?

Johan, an older German man, lowers the volume of the music and only then does Dwight look up.

> JOHAN
> He writes to me and says he misses me. He
> calls and says he loves me. And I reply,
> "I miss you too." But I don't.

Dwight gets up and moves from room to room, casually engrossed in the magazine.

> DWIGHT
> Maybe you don't know what you feel.

> JOHAN
> *(follows)*
> But I do know what I feel.

> DWIGHT
> *(stops and considers)*
> What time is your flight?

JOHAN
Seven o'clock.

DWIGHT
Is he going to meet you at the airport in New York?

JOHAN
Yes.

DWIGHT
What are you going to tell him?

JOHAN
What do you want me to tell him?

DWIGHT
I don't want to tell you what to do.

JOHAN
Then tell me what you want.

DWIGHT
That would be the same thing.

JOHAN
It would help me decide.

DWIGHT
He wants you to stay with him in New York?

JOHAN
Yes.

DWIGHT
(frustrated)
What do you want me to say?

JOHAN
I want you to tell me if there is a future for me and you.

DWIGHT
A future, huh?

JOHAN
Yes.

DWIGHT
(returns to magazine)
How can I answer that?

JOHAN
Yes or no.

Dwight drops the magazine and moves off.

DWIGHT
I can't see the future.

JOHAN
(calls after him)
You don't need to see it if you know it's there!

Dwight throws on a trendy new coat that still has the price tag on it. Tearing it off, he admires himself in the hallway mirror.

DWIGHT
Look, let me go get a car. I'll drive you out to the airport.

JOHAN
I can take a taxi.

DWIGHT
No. I want to. Can you wait here?

JOHAN
How long?

DWIGHT
An hour and a half.

                    JOHAN
　And then what?

Dwight comes and throws his arm around Johan.

                    DWIGHT
                  (buoyantly)
             Then I'll tell you the future!

                    JOHAN
                  (skeptical)
                 At five-thirty?

                    DWIGHT
　Without fail.

Johan considers this, shrugs, and reluctantly agrees.

                    JOHAN
　Okay. Five-thirty.

They kiss and Dwight leaves.

11. EXTERIOR, BERLIN—DAY

Exiting Johan's building, Dwight pauses again to admire his new coat. He strides away purposefully.

12. EXTERIOR, BERLIN—DAY

Dwight approaches a phone booth outside a train station. But just as he reaches it, a raunchy prostitute elbows her way past him and occupies the booth instead. The receiver is off the hook, dangling by its cord. Lifting it, she continues an earlier conversation.

                    WOMAN
              (into phone, in German)
               No. No. No. No?

Indignant, Dwight moves off to look for another phone. But he doesn't see one and so returns and waits.

                    WOMAN
              (continues, in German)
        No. No. No. No! I've run out of money. I'll
        call you back in a minute.

She hangs up. Dwight is waiting for her to vacate the booth. But she stays where she is and smiles.

                    WOMAN
              (continues, in German)
        My telephone card ran out. Can I use yours
        for a minute?

He just shrugs, not understanding her. She realizes and switches to English.

                    WOMAN
                 (continues)
        Can I use your phone card for just a minute?

She snatches his phone card out of his hand before he has time to reply.

                    DWIGHT
        Hey!

                    WOMAN
        I won't be long.

Fed up, Dwight turns and storms off.

                    DWIGHT
        Fine.

                    WOMAN
              (into phone, in German)
        It's me again. No. No?

Finally, Dwight changes his mind and walks back to confront her, pulling open the door to the booth and waiting with attitude. She smiles at him pleasantly and finishes her call.

> WOMAN
> *(continues, in German)*
> No. No. No. No. Okay. No. Bye.

She hangs up and hands Dwight back his phone card.

> WOMAN
> *(continues, in English)*
> Sorry.

> DWIGHT
> *(curt)*
> Don't worry about it.

> WOMAN
> Thank you.

> DWIGHT
> Yeah, right. See you around.

As she passes by, she reaches down and grabs his crotch.

> WOMAN
> *(winks)*
> Maybe.

She moves off. Dwight watches her go, offended, shocked, even a little entertained. Finally, he shakes his head clear, enters the booth, and dials. He waits and knocks some dust off his sleeve. Then—

> DWIGHT
> *(into phone)*
> Werner? It's me, Dwight. It's important. I need to ask you one question. I want you to tell me if there's a future for me and you.
> *(listens, then)*
> Yes or no.
> *(listens, impatient)*
> You don't need to see it if you know it's there. Meet at the bar in ten minutes.

13. INTERIOR, CAFE—DAY

As Dwight enters, the bartender, Mac, starts screaming at him.

> MAC
> *(in German)*
> You owe me money!

> DWIGHT
> *(oblivious)*
> Werner been in?

> MAC
> *(in German)*
> You do owe me money!

Dwight finds his friend, Elizabeth, surrounded by her entourage, three attractive young men striking cool and disinterested poses. One of them, Harry, is reading aloud from a book.

> HARRY
> *(in German)*
> "The Germans regard love as a virtue, a divine emanation, something mystical. It is not eager, impetuous, jealous and tyrannical, as it is in the heart of an Italian woman. It is deep, visionary, and utterly unlike anything in England."

Harry closes the book and smokes. The others, Tom and Dick, nod approvingly. Dwight barges into the middle of this and the entourage regard him with thinly veiled contempt.

> DWIGHT
> *(kisses her cheek)*
> Elizabeth, can I borrow your car? I've got to take Johan out to the airport.

> TOM
> *(sarcastic)*
> He's finally leaving you?

> DWIGHT
> He's just going away to New York because he's got some work to do there for three months.

Dick clears his throat and addresses Harry so that all can hear:

> DICK
> Have you heard the news?

> HARRY
> What news?

> DICK
> Werner left Greta.

They all look at Dwight whose eyes are wide with surprise.

> TOM
> *(to Elizabeth)*
> But do we know this for a fact?

> ELIZABETH
> I heard it from Simon.

Satisfied, Tom and Dick stand and wander away. Harry returns to his reading. Dwight sits with Elizabeth.

> DWIGHT
> Something happened between Werner and me.

> ELIZABETH
> *(not surprised)*
> Oh yeah? Like what?

> DWIGHT
> We got romantic.

> ELIZABETH
> *(amused)*
> Excuse me?

                    DWIGHT
Romantic.

Intrigued, Harry lowers his book.

                    HARRY
              (in German)
Romantic?

                    DWIGHT
We kissed.
              (then adds)
Once.

                    ELIZABETH
When?

                    DWIGHT
A few weeks ago.

                    HARRY
How?

Dwight lunges forward and kisses Harry on the mouth, causing the man to fall off his chair.

14. EXTERIOR, BERLIN—DAY

Dwight and Elizabeth approach her car which is parked down the street.

                    ELIZABETH
But what about Johan?

                    DWIGHT
              (sighs, annoyed)
Johan all of a sudden wants me to tell him
the future.

                    ELIZABETH
Johan is a remarkable man.

DWIGHT
Yeah, but Werner has always fascinated me too.

They reach her car and she hands him the keys.

ELIZABETH
I'd go for the sure thing.

DWIGHT
You would, huh?

ELIZABETH
Johan loves you. You love Johan.

DWIGHT
But he's going away to America for three months.

ELIZABETH
Well, don't you trust him?

DWIGHT
I'm already the guy he's seeing behind his boyfriend's back.

ELIZABETH
Yes, that's complicated. But then Werner is married to Greta.

DWIGHT
But he just left her.

ELIZABETH
That's true.

DWIGHT
But they could get back together again.

ELIZABETH
Happens all the time.

                    DWIGHT
               (sits into car)
          Unless I get in there now and make my play.

                    ELIZABETH
          It might be your only chance to know for
          sure.

He drives off.

15. INTERIOR, OLD MUSEUM—DAY

Some grand, old, but neglected palace is being renovated by construction workers. The men keep busy on scaffolding and pay no attention to the fashion photography shoot happening beneath them. A young female model is standing around in the nude waiting for the stylist, Simon, to return with the tiny dress she is to wear. He helps her into it as he berates Dwight.

                    SIMON
               (aggravated)
          Dwight, Werner is in a really complicated
          place in his life right now. He doesn't need to
          be getting mixed up with someone like you.

                    DWIGHT
          Someone like *me*? What's that supposed to
          mean?

                    SIMON
          You know what I mean.

                    DWIGHT
               (amused)
          No, I don't. What do you mean?

Simon pivots the model by her shoulders and studies the fall of the dress. He leads her off to the photographer. Dwight follows.

                    SIMON
          You're not serious.

DWIGHT
(rolls his eyes)
Serious. Like his wife, you mean?

SIMON
Greta is a pretty successful and well thought of woman most of the time.

DWIGHT
She's smothering him.

SIMON
Well, that's no reason for him to take up with an aimless flirt like you.

DWIGHT
Hey!

Simon delivers the model to the photographer and her assistants. They begin their work. Simon steps back to Dwight.

SIMON
You are with a different man every time I see you.

DWIGHT
(grins, flattered)
So, I'm lucky.

SIMON
(sighs impatiently)
You're not lucky, Dwight.
(walks away)
Du bist eine Schlampe.

DWIGHT
Eine Schlampe?

He takes out his pocket English-German dictionary and looks it up. Meanwhile, the photo shoot is moving on. Dwight and Simon follow with the model as the photographer and her assistants find a new tableau.

> DWIGHT
> *(continues)*
> What about Johan?

> SIMON
> What *about* Johan?

> DWIGHT
> I've been with Johan for six months and I haven't strayed once.

> SIMON
> *(furious)*
> So, what do you want me to do, give you a medal?!

Embarrassed by his outburst, Simon takes the model by her elbow and moves off. Dwight is perplexed.

> DWIGHT
> Are you upset?

> SIMON
> *(glances back)*
> Your problems are trivial.

The photo shoot marches off into the cavernous old building and Dwight is left alone. He lights a new cigarette and addresses three workmen who, as they are repairing part of the ceiling, have overheard this whole exchange.

> DWIGHT
> There's this man, right, Johan. He's great. We've been together for, like, six months. But now he's got to go to New York for three months and work. He's handsome. He's, you know... older. He's extremely intelligent and he's got excellent taste. He works very hard. He says he loves me, says he'll miss me, sure,

> but look, he's got this totally excellent
> ex-boyfriend back in New York; smart, good
> looking, successful... And, of course, he's a
> really nice guy too. Now, before Johan leaves
> Berlin—in an hour—he wants me to tell him
> if there's a future for us; for me and him. My
> question is this: am I wrong to want more time,
> more proof? Is it wrong of me to be scared?

He waits for a response but the workmen are impassive. Then he realizes the time, checks his wristwatch, tosses away his cigarette, and leaves in a hurry. The workmen watch him go, then (*in German*) thoughtfully discuss Dwight's dilemma.

BORIS
I think he's wrong.

PETER
You do?

BORIS
I don't know why he's scared. I think he
wants too much for too little.

MIKE
I think he has a legitimate reason for hesitating.
Besides his own indecision, this man, Johan,
has in fact shown himself to be capable of
infidelity; he's cheating on his lover in New York.

PETER
But then we don't know if Johan ever
displayed the same urge to commit to this
other man in New York the way he has with
Dwight.

BORIS
The point is: Dwight's been given an ultimatum.
He should know how he feels. He's acting in bad
faith. He wants the situation to remain ambiguous
indefinitely.

PETER

He's a flirt.

BORIS

(nods)

Exactly.

MIKE

(professorial)

But to flirt is to exist in ambiguity. Flirtation denotes nothing more or less than chaste amorous relations generally devoid of deep feelings. Yes, Dwight, like Bill in New York City, is a flirt. For people like this, to define what the situation really is between themselves and—well, the other—this is to destroy the very possibility of flirtation.

BORIS

So, what, are you standing up for him?

MIKE

For who?

BORIS

For Dwight?

MIKE

No. But I think Johan's ultimatum is a little exaggerated.

PETER

Perhaps Johan is quite fond of Dwight's flirtatiousness.

BORIS

But this isn't about flirtation. It's about seduction.

PETER

It's just a matter of degree, surely.

BORIS
(impatient)
He's trying to steal some woman's husband!

PETER
Ah, he's just having fun.

MIKE
You know, to seduce is, etymologically, to lead astray, to make someone take the wrong turn.

BORIS
You see, that sounds more like what's going on here.

PETER
Look, we don't know for sure if Werner is leaving his wife because Dwight kissed him.

BORIS
If we can believe what he is showing us, the filmmaker's project here has been to compare the changing dynamics of one situation in different milieus.

MIKE
And you don't think he'll succeed?

BORIS
Well, it's too early to tell, perhaps. But, no, I think he will fail.

PETER
(fascinated)
Yes, he will fail. He has already failed. But in this case the failure is interesting.

BORIS
(has had enough)
Why don't you just shut the fuck up.

> PETER
> *(insists)*
> The milieu is bound to change the dynamics
> of the situation!

> BORIS
> People are the same no matter what the
> milieu is!

They get back to work, lifting their tools and carrying them to the next patch of demolished ceiling.

> MIKE
> So, you don't think personality, character,
> has any effect on the situation?

> BORIS
> Stop twisting my words around.

> PETER
> The question, though, remains the same.
> What do you do when contingent reality
> demands a definitive response?

> BORIS
> We cannot exist in ambiguity forever!

Mike hangs back, though, considering this at length.

> MIKE
> I disagree. I think we can. Although I think
> it would be the deepest kind of isolation.

16. EXTERIOR, WERNER'S STUDIO—DAY

Dwight comes around the corner and parks. He gets out of the car before a typical East Berlin apartment house and strides confidently in through the entrance. He pauses in the courtyard where a little girl stops playing and regards him soberly. Dwight moves on and pushes in through a doorway on the right leading to a staircase. He glances back at the girl once more, then enters.

17. INTERIOR, WERNER'S STUDIO—DAY

Letting himself into the unlocked studio, Dwight is surprised to find Werner's wife, Greta, pacing forlornly amongst the stretched canvases and work tables covered with paint. He starts to turn away and leave, but she sees him. He stays. She pauses, then—

> GRETA
> *(in German)*
> Why is he doing this to me?

He doesn't know what she's asking and turns to leave again but is now blocked by the little girl who is between him and the door. Greta comes right up close behind him.

> GRETA
> *(continues, in English)*
> He loved me once. Why can't he love me now?

> DWIGHT
> People change.

> GRETA
> I don't change.

> DWIGHT
> Maybe you will.

> GRETA
> I don't want to change.

Dwight watches as Greta takes the little girl, her daughter, by the hand, sits her on a chair, and ties her shoelace. Then she sends the child away and sits in the chair herself.

> DWIGHT
> Look, Greta, nothing happened between me
> and Werner.

> GRETA
> But it might.

              DWIGHT
    No, it won't.

But he still wants to wait for Werner. So he tosses his coat aside, sits on the narrow daybed, and flips through some art magazines.

              GRETA
    Why isn't anything going to happen between
    you and Werner?

              DWIGHT
    I'm in love with Johan.

              GRETA
         (aside, in German)
    Liar.

              DWIGHT
    What?

              GRETA
    Do you ever think of settling down, Dwight?

              DWIGHT
         (preoccupied)
    Occasionally.

              GRETA
    Lately?

              DWIGHT
    A little.

              GRETA
    With Johan?

              DWIGHT
    Probably.

              GRETA
    He's a good man.

                    DWIGHT
                (blithely)
    Yes, he is.

                    GRETA
    Call him.

                    DWIGHT
                (confused)
    What?

                    GRETA
    Call him on the phone.

                    DWIGHT
    Why?

                    GRETA
    Call him!

Dwight drops the magazine and gestures for her to calm down. He crosses the studio and lifts the phone's receiver, dialing. He waits. Finally—

                    DWIGHT
    It's busy.

Not believing him, she stands and grabs the receiver. Hearing the busy signal, she slams it back down.

                    GRETA
    Damn!

Just as she is about to throw herself on the daybed, the phone rings. They both step back away from it, wary.

                    GRETA
                (continues)
    You answer it.

Dwight would rather not, but, sighing, he does.

                    DWIGHT
               (into phone)
          Hello?
               (relieved)
          Werner!
               (to Greta)
          It's Werner.
               (into phone)
          What? No. No. Don't worry about that. No.
          Really. Greta's here. You want to talk to her?
               (listens, then)
          No?

Dwight looks at the receiver in disbelief when Werner hangs up. He watches sadly as Greta, crushed, approaches a small bureau by the daybed and removes a handgun from the top drawer. She sits on the daybed and holds the weapon to her breast like a keepsake.

                    DWIGHT
          Now, what are you going to do with that?

                    GRETA
          I'm going to shoot myself.

                    DWIGHT
          That's pretty stupid, Greta.

                    GRETA
          Yeah, I guess I should shoot Werner, no?

Dwight comes over and sits on the daybed beside her, lightly massaging her back, consoling her.

                    DWIGHT
          No. You're not going to shoot anyone.

                    GRETA
          Maybe I should shoot you.

Just then, Dwight sees the little girl peeking around the edge of the door. He stands, crosses the room, and hands her his smokes and lighter.

                    DWIGHT
            Here, kid, go smoke my cigarettes.

The little girl runs away with them, curious and excited. Dwight turns back to Greta and considers the situation. Finally, he comes over, gently tips her chin up, leans down and kisses her on the mouth. Though surprised at first, she accepts it willingly. Dwight guides her back onto the daybed, kissing her still, and reaches out to remove the gun from her hand.

18. EXTERIOR, WERNER'S STUDIO—DAY

Werner himself comes staggering in from the sidewalk and into the courtyard, drunk. He finds his little girl trying to light a cigarette for herself. He lifts her in his arms and kisses her. Setting her back down, he goes inside and climbs the stairs. The child almost manages to light the cigarette when—Pow!!—the gun goes off upstairs. The child drops her new toys and presses herself back against the nearest wall. A neighbor passing through the courtyard stops as well and looks up at the studio. Greta now comes out, half-dressed, and finds her daughter. Then Dwight stumbles out holding his bleeding face. The neighbor screams when he falls to the pavement beside Elizabeth's car.

19. INTERIOR, HOSPITAL OPERATING ROOM—DAY

A female nurse is preparing the surgical instruments as an older male doctor inspects Dwight's injury.

                    DOCTOR
                (in German)
            This looks bad.
                (to nurse, turning away)
            Can you clean this, please?

The nurse approaches and begins swabbing Dwight's wounds with alcohol. Dwight is in shock and increasingly disturbed by the nurse and doctor's conversation which he cannot understand. The doctor stands back and considers the situation.

DOCTOR
(continues, in German)
I am going to give you something for the pain, but it is still going to hurt.

DWIGHT
(not understanding)
What?

DOCTOR
(in German)
Are you allergic to Novocaine?

DWIGHT
What's he saying?!

NURSE
Are you allergic to Novocaine?

DWIGHT
No.

NURSE
Nein.

DOCTOR
(in German)
Your upper lip is in three pieces. Can you feel that?

NURSE
Can you feel that?

DWIGHT
(desperate)
Feel what?!

DOCTOR
(in German)
You have two tears. One goes right up the side of your nose.

                    NURSE
              (translates)
You have two tears. One goes right up the
side of your nose.

                   DWIGHT
              (despondent)
Oh man...

                   DOCTOR
              (to nurse, in German)
Can he feel that?

                    NURSE
              (to Dwight)
Can you feel that?

                   DWIGHT
              (furious)
Yes!

Alarmed, the nurse steps aside and looks to the doctor for help. He comes forward, lays a hand on Dwight's shoulder, and attempts to speak English.

                   DOCTOR
Is your... breathing... troubled?

                   DWIGHT
No.

                   DOCTOR
Good. Okay.
              (turns away, in German)
Now, I must inject the Novocaine directly
into the wound. Okay?

                   DWIGHT
Okay. Whatever.

He lies back and waits for the worst.

                        DOCTOR
                    (to nurse, in German)
            I'm telling him this because it will not help
            if he does not know what is happening. I will
            need his help.

                        DWIGHT
            What's he saying?

The nurse decides not to translate and, coming around behind his head, soothes Dwight while the doctor prepares a needle.

                        NURSE
            Keep still.

                        DOCTOR
                        (in German)
            It's going to sting a bit.

The first injection causes Dwight to stiffen and groan, his hand gripping the table fiercely.

                        DOCTOR
            I know. I know… A few more…

                        NURSE
            Breathe.

                        DOCTOR
            Good. Now, on this side…

                        NURSE
            Just remember to breathe.

Finally, the doctor stands back, concerned.

                        DOCTOR
                        (in German)
            It is not doing any good. It is flowing right
            back out of the wounds. The Novocaine has
            nowhere to stay.

> *(then, to Dwight, in English)*
> Do you need to spit?

The nurse lightly presses a wad of gauze to the side of Dwight's face and allows him to drool into it. The doctor leans over and begins the stitching.

> NURSE
> Keep thinking about something. Something specific.

> DWIGHT
> I'm trying.

> NURSE
> Good. What are you thinking about?

> DWIGHT
> Guys.

> NURSE
> That's good. Tell me about the guys.

> DWIGHT
> *(slurs as doctor works)*
> Muscles... My hand on his ass... My cock in his hand... Kissing... His tongue in my mouth... My mouth on his chest... Spooning...

The doctor pauses in his work and looks to the nurse.

> DOCTOR
> "Spooning?"

> DWIGHT
> We lay side by side. My back to you. Your arm around my waist. We draw up our knees.

> DOCTOR
> *(concerned, in German)*
> What is he talking about?

The nurse decides not to answer.

> NURSE
> *(to Dwight, softly)*
> Keep still.

And the doctor returns to his work.

20. EXTERIOR, JOHAN'S BUILDING—NIGHT

Bandaged and missing his new coat, Dwight is on the sidewalk pressing the buzzer. But there is no answer. He steps out into the street and looks up at the darkened windows of the apartment.

21. EXTERIOR, IMBISS—NIGHT

Dwight counts out some coins he finds in his pocket and lays them on the high counter of this mobile kitchen by the roadside. The aproned woman in the truck looks at the money and shakes her head.

> WOMAN
> *(in German)*
> It's not enough for anything.

He retrieves his coins and stands off to the side, wrapping his arms around himself for warmth. A man, having a beer at the far end of the counter, is curious and, indicating the bandage on Dwight's face, asks:

> MAN
> *(in German)*
> What happened to you?

> DWIGHT
> I got shot by the wife of a man I thought I
> might be in love with.

The man nods and drinks his beer. Then he comes over, removes his jacket, and drapes it over Dwight's shoulders. Dwight is grateful and smiles. The man returns to the counter and his beer, gesturing that the young American should keep it. Dwight pushes his arms in to the sleeves and sighs, looking out at the passing traffic.

A title card announces: Tokyo, 1995

22. INTERIOR, DANCE SCHOOL—DAY

Miho, Yuki, and six male dancers are led through a rehearsal for a dance by their choreographer, a handsome older man, Ozu. The movement concerns the simple action of Miho approaching Yuki, who is curled up on the floor, and helping her to stand. Ozu moves amongst the dancers, directing them, sometimes demonstrating a gesture himself. He works particularly closely with Miho, attenuating her steps, conducting the rhythm of her movements. The other female dancer, Yuki, watches Ozu's attentive work with Miho jealously.

The short section of the piece is then executed by Miho and Yuki.

Then another section is rehearsed: the male dancers physically manipulate Miho, as if she were a puppet, so that she comes down over Yuki and embraces her while other dancers position Yuki's arms around Miho.

Later: the rehearsal over, everyone is preparing to leave. Ozu sits, preoccupied, and revises his notes.

23. INTERIOR, DANCE SCHOOL—DAY

Miho comes up the hallway in her regular street clothes but pauses when she hears a woman crying in the showers she is passing. She steps back and glances in.

Ozu is washing his hands at the sink while Yuki, crying, still in her costume, stands aside and holds a gun to her head. Unfazed, Ozu dries his hands, grabs the gun, and checks to see if it's loaded. Yuki grabs it back and smacks him in the face, causing Ozu to look towards the hallway where he sees Miho. Yuki does too. She storms out past Miho and runs off down the hall, terrifying some students who see the gun and duck for cover.

Finally, Ozu comes out into the hall and leans against the windows, distraught. Concerned, Miho steps over to a watercooler and gets him a drink. Grateful, he accepts it, drinks, then drops the paper cup and embraces Miho. She is startled and confused, but then, seeing he is crying, comfortingly hugs him in return. But then he tries to kiss her and she leans back away, alarmed. He pauses, holding her in his arms, and then succeeds in kissing her. She blinks in amazement. Finally, hearing a scuffle, they both look off at a nearby staircase where two of the male dancers, still in costume, and a young woman, Naomi, watch all this, stunned. They turn and go their separate ways.

Ozu snaps out of it, releases Miho, and walks off down the hall in the opposite direction.

24. INTERIOR, DANCE SCHOOL—DAY

Elsewhere, a few minutes later, Miho comes down another flight of stairs, passes through a doorway, and heads for the exit. She meets her friend, Naomi. *(Unless otherwise indicated, the language throughout is Japanese.)*

> NAOMI
> Miho, Ozu-san is in a complicated place in his life right now. He doesn't need to be getting mixed up with someone like you.
>
> MIHO
> Someone like me? What's that supposed to mean?
>
> NAOMI
> You know what I mean.
>
> MIHO
> No, I don't.
>
> NAOMI
> You're not serious.

Miho sits on a bench in the lobby and removes her hat.

                    MIHO
Serious like his wife, you mean.

                    NAOMI
            (joins her)
Yuki is a pretty successful and well thought
of woman most of the time.

                    MIHO
            (sadly)
She is smothering him.

                    NOAMI
Well that's no reason for him to take up with
an aimless flirt like you.

Miho is hurt. Naomi stands and leaves. Looking away, Miho sees a few of the male dancers, still in costume, watching from across the lobby.

25. EXTERIOR, EDIT ROOM—DAY

Miho comes up the crowded little street and stops to check her appearance in a shop window before entering the building.

26. INTERIOR, EDIT ROOM—DAY

A young American man, Hal, paces around the edit room while he talks on the phone. His assistant editor, Nagase, works at the rewinds. *(Dialogue is in English.)*

                    HAL
No. No.
            (holds his head, exhausted)
No! No.

Miho enters just as Hal hangs up the phone. She kisses him.

                    HAL
            (continues as he works)
I feel disgusting.

                        MIHO
Why?
            (as he doesn't answer)
What time is your flight?

                        HAL
Seven.

                        MIHO
Is she going to meet you at the airport in Los
Angeles?

                        HAL
Yes.

Miho sits and thinks. She glances at Nagase who looks away and busies himself with his work.

                        MIHO
             (softly, to Hal)
What do you want me to say?

                        HAL
I want you to tell me if there is a future for us.

                        MIHO
How can I answer that?

                        HAL
Yes or no.

                        MIHO
I can't see the future.

Hal stands, takes the screenplay off a shelf, flips through it, and finds the right line.

                        HAL
             (reads)
"You don't need to see it if you know it's
there."

Miho takes the screenplay from him and throws it in the garbage. Nagase looks over, concerned about the screenplay.

>   MIHO
> I'll go borrow Naomi's car and drive you to
> the airport.

>   HAL
> I can take a taxi.

>   MIHO
> No. I want to. Can you wait here?

>   HAL
> How long?

She checks the time on the wristwatch she wears, one much too large for her, a man's watch.

>   MIHO
> An hour and a half.

>   HAL
> And then what?

>   MIHO
> Then I will tell you the future.

>   HAL
> In an hour and a half?

>   MIHO
> I promise.

He takes her wrist and looks at the time on her watch.

>   HAL
> At five-thirty?

>   MIHO
> Without fail.

                    HAL
        Okay. Five-thirty.

They kiss and she leaves. Nagase watches her go and then, when the door is closed, turns to Hal.

                    NAGASE
        You owe me money, man.

                    HAL
        I owe lots of people money.

27. EXTERIOR, EDIT ROOM—DAY

Miho exits the building and approaches a pay phone. She inserts her card and dials. Nagase comes out, passes her, and feeds money into a vending machine that sells cans of beer. He overhears Miho's call.

                    MIHO
                (into phone)
        Ozu-san? It's me, Miho. It's important. I need
        to ask you one question. I want you to tell me
        if there is a future for me and you.
                (waits, listens, then)
        Yes or no.
                (listens again, then)
        You don't need to see it if you know it's there.
        Okay. I will see you in ten minutes.

She hangs up and, not noticing Nagase, heads up the street.

28. INTERIOR, DANCE SCHOOL—DAY

Miho comes up the hall and knocks on Ozu's office door. There is no response. Naomi passes by.

                    MIHO
                (calls)
        Naomi, can I borrow your car? I have to
        drive Hal to the airport.

NAOMI
(cruel)
He's finally leaving you, huh?

Hurt once again, Miho moves off and sits in a stairwell.

MIHO
He is just going to Los Angeles for three
months to do some work he has there.

Now Naomi feels bad. She joins Miho and hands her the keys to her car.

NAOMI
Don't you trust him?

MIHO
I'm already the girl he is seeing behind his
girlfriend's back.

Naomi nods, understanding, but without sympathy. She stands and leaves. As she goes out, she passes two policemen entering, an older man named Mochi and a much younger kid named Tomo. They march up the stairs right past Miho, Tomo doffing his cap politely to her as he passes. She watches them till they disappear on the floor above then, startled, discovers Yuki, still in her costume—makeup running—sitting right there beside her.

YUKI
(whispers)
Why is he doing this to me?

MIHO
(also whispers)
I don't know.

YUKI
He loved me once. Why can't he love me now?

MIHO
People change.

                    YUKI
I don't change.

                    MIHO
Maybe you will.

                    YUKI
I don't want to change.

                    MIHO
Sometimes you have no choice.

                    YUKI
Do you change?

                    MIHO
I'm changing all the time.

                    YUKI
That's why all the men like you so much.

                    MIHO
The men don't all like me so much.

                    YUKI
My husband likes you.

Miho now looks right at Yuki, unsure what the woman means. Then Ozu comes up the hall and grabs his wife by the arm. He struggles to get the gun away from her. He succeeds and pauses, listening to the two cops moving about on an upper floor. He wonders what to do with the weapon. Finally, he looks at Miho, removes her hat, and hides the gun inside it. He motions for her to leave quickly. After a moment's confusion, she does so. Ozu mounts the stairs to deal with the cops while Yuki drifts towards the exit, following Miho.

29. EXTERIOR, DANCE SCHOOL—DAY

Miho jumps out the door into an alley at the back of the school. She moves along, looking for a place to dispose of the weapon.

Finding a long row of garbage cans against the opposite wall, she drops her hat containing the gun in one of them and hurries off. But then she stops, realizing she still wants her hat. She goes back and retrieves it but then sees an elderly homeless man digging around in the garbage further along. Concerned, she reaches in and takes the gun out again, setting off to look for a safer place to ditch it.

A moment later, she innocently steps out into a busy side street with the gun held out in full view, searching for a better hiding place. A mature couple come face to face with her and, seeing the gun, fall back in terror. Miho realizes, hides the gun behind her back, and smiles sweetly before running off down another alley.

30. EXTERIOR, ANOTHER ALLEY—DAY

Miho finds herself alone and, apparently, not followed. Desperate, she looks around and finds a bicycle leaning up against the back wall of a little restaurant. She tosses the gun into the basket on the bike's handlebars and runs off. But Yuki has followed. The troubled woman emerges from the shadows at the end of the alley and approaches the gun.

31. EXTERIOR, MAIN STREET—DAY

Miho runs along through different backstreets and suddenly finds herself out on a large main road filled with people and shops. But still worried, she enters a bookstore.

32. INTERIOR, BOOKSTORE—DAY

She enters and goes directly in amongst the shelves, trying to mix in with the crowd. She drifts from section to section, aisle to aisle, idly flipping through books and magazines, keeping an eye on the entrance to see if she has been followed. One of the books she picks up at random, however, interests her, and she quietly reads to herself as she moves along.

            MIHO
         (reads)
    "Love is an actual thing. We ourselves bring

> it into existence. These words, these written pages, the melody of the sentences, the images they conjure—these are not just the products of love, nor are they merely the expression of love. They are a form love has taken. They are, actually, my love."

Moved, she stops and reflects on this. Then she looks up and sees everyone watching her. The mature couple she frightened on the street are pointing her out to the two cops she saw at the school.

33. EXTERIOR, ANOTHER ALLEY—DAY

The cops, Mochi and Tomo, lead Miho back to where she hid the gun. A small crowd has gathered and follows along. They find the bicycle, but when they search through its basket, they do not find the gun. Miho is dismayed. They march her off and put her into the backseat of their squad car.

34. EXTERIOR, EDIT ROOM—DAY

Nagase is loading the trunk of a taxicab with bulky metal film canisters. Hal is getting them some beers at the vending machine.

> NAGASE
> *(in English)*
> Hal, come on. It's time to go.

> HAL
> Has Miho been back?

> CAB DRIVER
> *(in Japanese)*
> You owe me money!

Hal looks to Nagase for a translation.

> NAGASE
> *(ignores the driver)*
> Hal, man, Miho is with a different guy every time I see her.

                    HAL
              (hands him a beer)
So, she's lucky.

                  NAGASE
She's not lucky, man. She's loose.

                    HAL
Loose?

                  NAGASE
Loose.

                    HAL
What about me?

                  NAGASE
What about you?

                    HAL
I've been with Miho for, like, six months and
she hasn't strayed once.

                  NAGASE
              (unimpressed)
So what!

Hal drags a thick stack of yen from his pocket and hands it to Nagase who stands aside and counts it as the director is driven off in the taxicab.

35. INTERIOR, POLICE STATION—DAY

Mochi interrogates Miho as Tomo gets her a drink of water.

                  MOCHI
What's the matter? Are you upset?
         (she nods and he turns away)
Your problems are trival.

Miho takes the cup of water from Tomo, drinks, then addresses the younger policeman.

> MIHO
> Something happened between my teacher
> and me.

> TOMO
> *(kindly)*
> Yeah, like what?

> MIHO
> We kissed. Once.

Tomo looks away, shyly. But Mochi has heard enough.

36. INTERIOR, HOLDING CELL—DAY

Tomo leads Miho to the cell and locks her in with three other young women: a traditional housewife in a kimono, Narumi, a tense businesswoman, Shoko, and a sullen punk rocker, Kazuko. The three of them sit in silence, watching Miho where she stands just inside the door, until she feels she needs to explain.

> MIHO
> My boyfriend and I have been together for
> six months. But now he has to travel to Los
> Angeles for three months to work. He says
> he loves me and that he will miss me very
> much. But there is another woman in Los
> Angeles, his ex-girlfriend, who wants to
> marry him. She is beautiful, successful, and
> intelligent. She is a nice person. Before he
> leaves, he wants me to tell him if there is a
> future for us—for me and him.
> *(comes closer)*
> Am I wrong to hesitate? Is it wrong of me
> to want more time? More proof? Is it wrong
> of me to be so scared?

The three women remain silent a moment, considering. Then they all start speaking at once.

KAZUKO
Fuck him!

SHOKO
Don't let him go!

NARUMI
Nobody's perfect. We're all incomplete.

KAZUKO
He's manipulating you.

SHOKO
He'll get away.

NARUMI
We have to understand the people we love had lives before meeting us.

KAZUKO
Who the hell does he think he is—a gift from God?!

SHOKO
Yes, you were wrong to want more time.

NARUMI
They have histories.

KAZUKO
Tell him to get lost!

NARUMI
And their time with us is a separate history.

SHOKO
You won't be young forever.

KAZUKO
This jerk leaving Japan is the best thing that ever happened to you!

                    NARUMI
               (looks away, sadly)
          We're all banged up and broken. It's
          embarrassing.

                    KAZUKO
          Fuck him!

Finally, Tomo returns and escorts Miho away.

37. INTERIOR, POLICE STATION—NIGHT

Miho is given back her belongings and is released. As she puts on her wristwatch, she sees the time and is worried. It's six o'clock. She finds a pay phone in the lobby and dials frantically.

38. INTERIOR, EDIT ROOM—NIGHT

Nagase is still counting his money. The phone rings and interupts his progress.

                    NAGASE
               (answers, aggravated)
          Yeah. No. He's gone.

He hangs up and starts counting all over again.

39. INTERIOR, POLICE STATION—NIGHT

Depressed, Miho wanders away from the pay phone just as Mochi and Tomo return to the station with Ozu. They attempt to speak, but the policemen usher the teacher into another room and close the door.

40. EXTERIOR, POLICE STATION—NIGHT

Miho comes out onto the busy street and wonders what to do now. Putting on her jacket, she finds the keys to Naomi's car in the pocket. Suddenly more optimistic, she steals a bike leaning unlocked against a nearby shop and rides off. Mochi and Tomo are watching from a distance. They follow.

41. EXTERIOR, DANCE SCHOOL—NIGHT

Miho reaches the school, drops the bike in the road and rushes towards Naomi's car. But just as she is about to unlock the driver's side door, she sees one of Hal's film canisters, tipped over on its side, lying on the pavement just outside the entrance to the school. She comes over and confirms what it is. Then, assuming Hal must be inside, sighs with relief, lifts the canister, and enters.

42. INTERIOR, DANCE SCHOOL—NIGHT

Entering, Miho stops and listens. The school seems to be empty. Curious, she climbs the stairs to the second floor and pauses again. There seems to be no one around. She comes up the hall and stops outside the rehearsal studio where they worked earlier in the day. Yuki is asleep in a chair, disheveled, still in her make-up and costume. Miho quietly places the film canister down on the tiled floor of the hallway and approaches carefully, seeing the gun on the floor by Yuki's foot along with a half-empty bottle of whiskey.

Meanwhile, Mochi and Tomo return to the school and enter the deserted lobby.

Miho comes down over Yuki, reaching out to grasp the gun. Just as she is about to touch it, though, Yuki's hand darts out and grabs her wrist. Startled, Miho stops. Then she just grabs it with her free hand instead. She tries to get back out to the hallway but Yuki hangs on her and drags her back. Finally, Miho manages to shake her off and Yuki falls to the floor, looking up at Miho in anger. Miho stares Yuki down and holds the weapon to her own head. Yuki is shocked, suddenly afraid and ashamed. She starts crying again.

Mochi reaches the second-floor landing and pauses, thinking he hears someone. Tomo, preoccupied, follows at a distance.

Back in the studio, Miho relaxes and lowers the gun from her head. She comes down to Yuki and embraces her just as she did in the dance rehearsal earlier. But she has forgotten she is still holding the gun which is now pointing directly at her own face.

Out in the hall, Mochi steps around the suspicious film canister and sees the two women in the studio. Tomo catches up, sees the film canister and, curious, gives it a little kick, tipping it over. The smack of metal against the floor startles the women, the gun goes off, and Miho is thrown back. Yuki looks on in horror.

43. INTERIOR, EMERGENCY ROOM—NIGHT

In a busy and noisy emergency room, a doctor and nurse work quickly to help Miho, who is laid out on the table, panicked and jumpy.

> DOCTOR
> *(to nurse)*
> This is bad. Wipe all this away.

He steps away to prepare an injection, troubled, as the nurse tries to clean the wound.

> DOCTOR
> *(continues, to Miho)*
> I'm going to give you something for the pain.
> But this is going to be painful anyway.

> NURSE
> *(to Miho, calming her)*
> Breathe.

> DOCTOR
> *(approaches)*
> I'm going to have to inject the painkiller
> directly into the wounds.

> NURSE
> Just remember to breathe.

> DOCTOR
> *(leans in with needle)*
> There will be a number of injections.

With the first injection, Miho screams loudly and starts kicking and struggling to escape.

> NURSE
> Breathe.

> DOCTOR
> Listen! I know! I know! But I can't put you
> out! I need you to cooperate!

> NURSE
> *(in Miho's ear)*
> Think about something. Something specific.

44. INTERIOR, BEDROOM—DAY

(*Intercut with previous scene*) Miho remembers a man's hand caressing her thigh tenderly. But—

The doctor is increasingly distressed and leans back.

> DOCTOR
> This is very bad.

> NURSE
> *(calls off)*
> More gauze!

Meanwhile, in Miho's mind, another man, on some other day, leans down and kisses her neck.

> DOCTOR
> Your entire upper lip is in three pieces. Can
> you feel that? One of the tears goes right
> across your cheek. You can feel that, can't you?

Now Miho pulls back the bedsheets to admire the body of some handsome young man some years earlier. Meanwhile—

> DOCTOR
> *(losing confidence)*
> The painkiller is running right out of the

wounds. There's no place for it to stay.

> NURSE
> *(to Miho)*
> That's painkiller in your mouth right now.
> Not blood. Do you need to spit?

But Miho is now remembering Hal in bed, sleeping with his arms around her as she lies awake. She smiles when she sees he is still wearing his wristwatch. She removes it and puts it on her own wrist.

45. INTERIOR, EMERGENCY ROOM—NIGHT

Some time later, it's all over. Miho is sitting on the edge of the operating table with her face bandaged, waiting for the strength to get up and leave.

46. INTERIOR, HOSPITAL LOBBY—NIGHT

She comes down a hallway and finds a pay phone. She takes out her calling card and lifts the receiver, but pauses, not sure who to call. Then she looks away, thinking, and discovers Hal asleep in a seat in the waiting room, surrounded by his film canisters. She comes over and watches him sleep. Finally, she lifts a film canister off the seat beside him, places it on the floor, and sits beside Hal herself. She lifts his arm and drapes it over her shoulders. Still, he doesn't wake up. But in his light sleep, he feels her close and holds her to himself. Miho closes her eyes and rests.

~ The End

www.ingramcontent.com/pod-product-compliance
Lightning Source LLC
Chambersburg PA
CBHW071241070526
44583CB00017B/2274